YOU CAN FIND TRUE LOVE

THE ESSENTIAL GUIDE TO MEETING THE LOVE OF YOUR LIFE

JESSICA WEI, M.D.

Difference Press

McLean, Virginia, USA

Copyright © Jessica Wei, M.D., 2021

All rights reserved. No part of this book may be reproduced in any form without permission in writing from the author. Reviewers may quote brief passages in reviews.

Published 2021

DISCLAIMER

Throughout this book, I have used some examples from my clients' personal lives. However, to ensure privacy and confidentiality, I have not included their names and have changed some of the details of their experience. None of the personal examples of my own life have been altered.

The author of this book does not dispense medical advice or prescribe the use of any technique as a form of treatment for physical, emotional, or medical problems without the advice of a physician, either directly or indirectly. The intent of the author is only to offer information of a general nature to help you in your quest for emotional, physical, and spiritual well-being. If you use you use any of the information in this book for yourself, the author and the publisher assume no responsibility for your actions.

Neither the author nor the publisher assumes any responsibility for errors, omissions, or contrary interpretations of the subject matter herein. Any perceived slight of any individual or organization is purely unintentional.

Brand and product names are trademarks or registered trademarks of their respective owners.

No part of this publication may be reproduced or transmitted in any form or by any means, mechanical or electronic, including photocopying or recording, or by any information storage and retrieval system, or transmitted by email without permission in writing from the author.

Cover Design: Jennifer Stimson

Editing: Erika Parsons

Author Photo Credit: Jane Shauck Photography

*For Ben and David,
my ever-happy, ever-kind, and ever-wise children.
Thank you for showing me how true love manifests every day.*

CONTENTS

1. Why Is It So Hard to Find Lasting Love?	1
2. How Did I Finally Find True Love?	9
3. How Can You Find True Love?	19
4. The First Essential Step to Finding True Love: Slow Down	27
5. Align Your Body and Mind to Find True Love	35
6. How We Prevent Ourselves from Finding True Love	47
7. Learning to How to Find True Love	57
8. Defining the Boundaries of True Love	69
9. Practice True Love While Dating	79
10. Practice True Love with Yourself Every Day	89
11. Still Not Sure You Can Find True Love?	97
12. You Can Find True Love at Long Last!	103
Acknowledgments	109
About the Author	111
About Difference Press	113
Other Books by Difference Press	115
Thank You	117

WHY IS IT SO HARD TO FIND LASTING LOVE?

"To love oneself is the beginning of a lifelong romance."

— Oscar Wilde

Our three and five-year-old sons were sleeping soundly in their beds. That night, I sat down to have what I hoped would be a heart-to-heart conversation with my husband. We had been having challenges with communication and connection from two months into knowing each other, and we had now been unhappily married for six years. After eighteen months of weekly couples' therapy, I was feeling beyond worn out and discouraged. While I wanted desperately to preserve our marriage, I knew that it was irreconcilably broken and over.

We were sitting on the opposite ends of the couch, wordlessly watching some television show I can't remember. I distinctly remember feeling so disconnected from this man with whom I once had shared the dream of creating a beautiful family and life. What had happened?

"Do you mind turning off the TV so we can talk?" I asked haltingly, not sure that he would answer.

He turned his head slowly toward me. "What? What do you want to talk about now?"

"This isn't working. None of this is working. We've been going to see Monica for therapy every week for over a year and a half, and I feel as if we've gotten nowhere. I think that things are getting worse, day by day." I paused here to listen for a reply. Silence. No reply. And then, the wide gap of more silence.

I pressed on. "The truth is that I feel like I am my worst version of myself when I am with you and that you are likewise the worst version of yourself when you are with me. I don't know how to make this better, and we've both been trying very hard. Don't you think that maybe we need to end this struggle with each other?"

More deafening silence. An empty blank stare, with a pair of cold steel-blue eyes blinking back at me. I feel my heart sinking to the pit of my belly, with all-too-familiar anxiety rising and pounding in my chest and head.

"I don't know what you're saying to me right now," he finally replied. "I think we need to keep trying. I don't want to get divorced. I want to keep trying. To me, this marriage isn't over yet."

And so, yet again, I felt thrust into a whirlwind of confusion and indecision. Despite what he said, I moved out of the bedroom that night to sleep on a mattress on the floor in the spare bedroom. We never slept together again. I was almost completely overwhelmed with the responsibilities of taking care of my patients in a hectic private Ob-Gyn practice while raising two toddler sons. I needed a very wide and deep berth of space.

That summer, I decided to train for a hundred-mile road bike ride. I trained with my friends on many days, and often I would ride up to fifty miles in a day, alone. There was plenty of open space and time to reflect on what to do next. And eight days after completing the century ride and 1,500 miles on the road on my trusted Trek carbon-fiber bike, I served my husband with divorce papers. I was upstairs in the spare bedroom when the doorbell rang, and I heard him receive the official documents from the state marshal. Tears filled my eyes. I felt crushed and heartbroken, but I knew it was what I needed to do.

There are *too* many stories of divorce and heartbreak. Mine is only one of the millions of stories. I am using divorce as one marker for the breakup of a long-term relationship. Many people in long-term relationships do not marry. I am generally referring to the dream of spending the rest of your life with someone and having that dream break down and end terribly. The number of marriages and divorces is measurable, and so what do the statistics tell us?

Marriage and divorce statistics from 2018, according to the Centers for Disease Control and Prevention (CDC), reveal these findings:

- Number of marriages in 2018: 2, 132,853
- Marriage rate: 6.5 per 1,000 total population
- The number of divorces in 2018: 782, 038 (in forty-five reporting states and D.C.)
- Divorce rate: 2.9 per 1,000 population (in forty-five reporting states and D.C.)

The overall divorce rate is around 50 percent. According to the National Center for Family and Marriage Research (NCFMR), that figure rises to 60 percent for second marriages and 65 percent for third and fourth marriages.

The average first marriage that ends in divorce lasts about eight years. Stated in a much more dramatic and sobering way:

- Every thirteen seconds, there is one divorce completed in the United States.
- That equates to 227 divorces per hour; 6,646 per day.
- There are nine divorces in the average of two minutes that it takes for a couple to recite their wedding vows.

What are the reasons individuals commonly cite for getting divorced? According to a study published in 2013 by researchers at the University of Denver:

- Lack of commitment: 75 percent
- Infidelity or extramarital affairs: 59.6 percent
- Too much conflict and arguing: 57.7 percent
- Getting married too young: 45.1 percent
- Financial problems: 36.7 percent
- Substance abuse: 34.6 percent
- Domestic violence: 23.5 percent
- Health problems: 18.2 percent
- Lack of support from family: 17.3 percent
- Religious differences: 13.3 percent
- Little or no premarital education: 13.3 percent

When asked who is to blame for the divorce, about 75 percent said that the other person was to blame due to infidelity, substance abuse, and/or domestic violence. Participants were also asked whether they felt that their partner should have worked harder to save their marriage. 65.8 percent of men and 73.8 percent of women believed that their ex-spouse should have made more effort to keep the marriage intact.

I share these findings to highlight the fact that so many people are looking for lasting, true love through marriage, only to find themselves disillusioned and divorced in the end. The statistics alone are heartbreaking and sad. Many people are looking for true love, and too many people do not find the lasting love they want and deserve.

WHAT FRUSTRATES US ABOUT DATING AND FINDING LOVE?

When I talk with my divorced friends about finding another romantic relationship, some have simply given up. Gone are the days of quickly meeting someone in person and feeling and building that special connection. Since we are no longer young, like when we easily met people in high school, college, and in young adulthood, the prospects for finding that lasting relationship often seem grim and slim. Add to that the often-traumatizing experiences of endless conflict, the fighting, the repeated disappointments, and heartache of broken relationships. It is, then, no surprise that for many of us, it is challenging to find that true, lasting love of a lifetime. Modern online dating provides a seemingly more accessible way to meet people, yet most of us find it baffling, disheartening, and fruitless. These dating sites offer so many faces and profiles from which to choose the perfect mate – shouldn't it be easy to find someone?

Over the years, many of my patients have shared with me their stories of love and loss. I have been privileged to take care of thousands of women through the journeys of their pregnancies and deliveries. I have met with them and their partners for dozens of prenatal appointments and spent hours with them during the labor and delivery of their babies. Remembering these very precious moments shared with so many couples brings me great joy. And sometimes, patients would come in for their annual gynecologic exam with the devastating news of getting divorced. In the years afterward, we would sometimes commiserate about the difficulties of dating after divorce, now with the responsibilities of being single mothers and working.

Laura is one of my patients who shared a great deal of her story with me. She has been divorced for over seven years. She thought that she would be happily remarried by now, and she isn't. She has had several excellent long-term relationships, none of which have worked out. With each relationship, she quickly identified all that she appreciated and loved about the men she was with, and they were almost what she wanted each time. It seemed that none of them were as available and connected to her as she wanted. They all seemed to be *almost* the right guy, but then not entirely.

One year during her annual visit, she burst into tears soon after I entered the exam room. "Dr. Wei! What am I doing wrong? I'm attractive, fit, smart, a great mother to my kids, successful, creative, active, and funny. I feel like I have everything it takes to be a great partner to a good man. When I'm in a relationship, I do everything for my man: cook, clean, organize, and do anything that he needs me to do. I am so available to him, and I get so frustrated because it seems like he isn't available to me in the same way. I end up feeling frustrated and deprived of attention and love. I just want to find the one, and it seems like he's not out there. I'm terrified that after the kids leave for college, I will be living my life alone. I just don't get it. I meet great men who are attractive, sexy, healthy, intelligent, and active. Everything seems to go so well for the first few months. I've felt more than a few times that I have met the one that I wanted to spend the rest of my life with. In the moment, the relationship seems like the one I have been looking for. Yet, even when I give everything I have in my heart, it just seems like it's not enough. I feel anxious so much of the time, and I feel as if I want him to give more. So many times, I want to say to him, *why don't you give me the attention I deserve? The love that I deserve?* Sometimes, I feel so angry when he disappears and doesn't answer my texts and phone calls. Even when I tell him that this hurts my feelings, he says he understands, and then still nothing changes. In the end, I just want so much more. Are all men just idiots?"

Then she paused to take a breath, and finished by saying, "I know that I spend too much time and energy thinking about this. When I am in a relationship, I never really feel relaxed within the relationship, so I spend a lot of time and energy worrying about getting what I want and need. If I could just find the right man and relationship, I could relax and devote that time and energy to the projects I want to focus on and get done. I don't want to feel deprived and anxious all of the time."

I gave her a much-needed hug. I told her that I understand what she has shared with me, and it isn't too different from what I hear from many of my divorced patients and friends.

Maybe you can relate to some of what she shared with me. Why is it so hard to find lasting love? Why does divorce occur so often? Is there something wrong with you? Is that why you can't find true love? Do you wonder if you are enough and have enough to find true love? And is it possible that you separated from yourself and divorced yourself long before you married and divorced another? Let's explore this a bit more in the coming chapters. First, I'll share with you my story of repeated attempts and losses in the search for true love.

2

HOW DID I FINALLY FIND TRUE LOVE?

"Real love doesn't make you suffer. How could it?
It doesn't suddenly turn into hate, nor does real joy turn into pain.
As I said, even before you are enlightened —
before you have freed yourself from your mind —
you may get glimpses of true joy, true love,
or of a deep inner peace, still but vibrantly alive."

— Eckhart Tolle,
The Power of Now

ALWAYS ON THE HUNT FOR LOVE

"Why are you always looking for a man and a romantic relationship?" My mother asked me this repeatedly after I left my husband. I had immediately hopped onto an online dating site soon after moving out of the house. I met the first man I would date after my now second marriage and divorce.

I never really knew how to answer my mother, and I never felt that she had the right to ask me this question. After all, she had been married to my father for over forty years. Their marriage wasn't the happiest, but neither of them left. Since I consider myself a *hopeless romantic*, I felt as if I genuinely needed another person in my life to have adventures with and to move through life with. What was wrong with that? I also knew that I felt much safer when I was in a relationship, even though I also always experienced more intermittent anxiety while in a relationship. Because I could never control whether the other person would maintain their attention and love for me, I would often worry about keeping things going well, or what I perceived as *well*.

THE FIRST ATTEMPT AT LOVE AFTER DIVORCE

I was still in the midst of my career as an Ob-Gyn and now a single mother of two elementary school-aged children. I deserved to have a break and have fun, right? Of course, I did! Alex and I first met after my divorce. I felt immediate fireworks during our first date. As we left the restaurant, he placed his hand on the small of my back to guide me outside, where we embraced and kissed. I had been feeling so starved for affection and touch that I melted into his arms. It felt *so* good. Raindrops started to fall on both of our faces, so we retreated to his sporty, cherry red BMW 330xi, where we proceeded to make out wildly for two hours.

So began a three-year relationship with a man with whom I enjoyed so many interests and great times. We ran together and completed many races, including the Marine Corps Marathon. We traveled, cooked, shared many delicious meals, and enjoyed visiting vineyards and wine tastings. He started a small vineyard on his family's farmland, and we took care of the grapes together, harvested them, and made delicious wine. There was so much that we enjoyed together. Yet, from the beginning, he told me that he never could commit to being with me long-term because my sons were so much younger than his, by eight years. Because I was having more fun with him than I ever had with any man, I always answered, "I only want you to be happy. I understand why you are saying that." Then, I held my breath for the next three years, hoping that he would change his mind, that he would love me enough to forget about this pronouncement that he could never commit to me long-term.

Meanwhile, I was facing different work challenges, including the most challenging month of my career as an Ob-Gyn, March 2011. Our relationship was increasingly strained, and we would intermittently take breaks to date other people, only to get back together a few weeks later.

THE SECOND ATTEMPT

After Alex and I finally ended things for good, I went through a series of long-term relationships. The first was with a super-talented, but volatile, writer and high school English teacher who lived in northern Vermont. During that long, drawn-out, four-year relationship, I never felt completely safe. Still, I stayed because he seemed to adore me and would stay with me through the thick and thin of my stressful work life and the sometimes-serious depression and anxiety with which I continued to struggle. I felt loved, even though I never loved him. He eventually became impatient to see the *new and improved* Jessie appear, the one who was free of hang-ups and mood swings. After much gnashing of teeth and terrible arguments, I ended that relationship after a year of barely seeing each other at all. I did not know how to choose partners well, and I certainly didn't understand how to be in a healthy relationship. I just knew that I wanted to be loved and cared for and to feel safe.

THE THIRD ATTEMPT AND FOURTH ATTEMPT

I met Oliver a few months after leaving my job as an Ob-Gyn in May 2016. He was handsome, charming, and calming to me. A few days after we met, he took me out to try sport kayaking at a local river with rapids. I had gone kayaking before, so I thought that trying this would be no big deal. As I donned all of the safety gear at the shore, he smiled and reassured me that this area was a relatively safe place to practice getting into the water. So, I paddled into the water slowly. Before I understood what was happening, I was swept up into what was probably a tiny rapid for experienced kayakers but was completely unfamiliar territory for me. The kayak flipped upside down, and I found myself massively disoriented and tossed about by the water rushing around me. Suddenly, I felt strong arms wrapped around my torso, lifting me out of the water to apparent safety. I had an immediate visceral reaction of feeling so safe in this shallow water rescue.

He was a leader with a local Tibetan Buddhist community, which I soon joined and was helped so much from my connection with my teachers. However, I seemed to believe that Oliver could do no wrong and that he would make me a better and more stable person. It was as if I was in a complete trance. However, he was swamped and overwhelmed with work and his volunteer leadership with this Buddhist group, so he wasn't as available as I wanted him to be. I officially broke off our relationship after eight months, shortly after opening my women's holistic functional medicine practice. I would continue to believe that I was safe, protected, and at home in Oliver's arms, and cared long after I had broken off my relationship with him.

Although I still yearned to be with Oliver, I also thought I should move on by getting back onto the online dating site to meet another person. Soon after this foray back, I met Warren, who was kind, gentle, and more attentive to me than anyone had ever been. He lived in a cute little house near the Long Island Sound. I knew from the beginning that I didn't feel much chemistry with him. Despite everything, Oliver still had me hooked. I quickly moved forward with dating Warren because it felt good to be in constant contact with someone who was so attracted to me and liked me so much. Of course, it didn't last long. Like a flash in the pan, it was over before it began. In my heart, I wished I had felt that spark that is so necessary for ongoing connection in a romantic relationship, but I didn't. Warren is a kind, generous, and loving man, and he deserved to be with someone who could return the care that he so lovingly gave. Perhaps I wasn't yet ready to receive that kind of love.

THE FIFTH ATTEMPT

After this, I took an eighteen-month break from dating. I understood that my lack of success in keeping relationships going had something to do with a lack of a sense of intrinsic value and worthiness. I had grown up in a confusing environment where I often didn't feel safe or loved, although my parents did love me very much and took good care of me materially.

I started to focus all my energies on developing my business and taking care of patients. I became involved with a powerful, functional medicine mentorship group, a public speaking coaching group, and a book coaching program. This led me to write my first book, *Physician, Care for Thyself*. I was determined to help as many people as possible through my medical practice, speaking, and writing. I felt incredibly inspired and energized by the people I was meeting and the work that I was doing.

During this tremendous professional growth period, I met Mark, who lived in one of the most beautiful communities along the shoreline of Connecticut. We met for coffee in my hometown. I liked him almost at once. He handed me the gift of a book, *Standing at the Edge: Finding Freedom Where Fear and Courage Meet,* by Roshi Joan Halifax. I had this feeling that he already knew me well after reading that fantastic book. How did he know what I needed to read at that critical time in my life when I was taking great leaps of faith in my work life?

When I first visited his rental house, just footsteps from the water, I noticed many things that I took as *signs* that he was the One: the broccoli sprouts that he had growing in three Mason jars in his dish drainer; the Berkey water filter I had been thinking about buying soon; and that on his bookshelf he owned many of the same spiritual titles I owned. I also ignored most of what bothered me about his messy and barely furnished house. I assumed that the furniture must have come with the rental because there was no way that he owned this old-fashioned wooden furniture with worn plaid cushions. We quickly fell for each other and soon afterward made plans to travel to Sedona together to attend a spiritual conference together. How could this be wrong?

The first few months felt fun, connected, and right. I loved spending the summer by the water and watching the sunset with him most nights of the week. We enjoyed doing so many things together: cooking and eating well, taking care of our physical health and bodies, meditating, and practicing yoga. We shared delicious dinners at our favorite restaurants where the waitstaff would assume we were a long-time married couple. In so many ways, I felt at home with him. At the same time, I also felt that I couldn't entirely be myself around him. Over time, I began to hide any difficulty with stress, my work, or other pressures. He wanted to be with the bright and sexy version of Jessie. I wanted to be the bright and sexy version of me! I tried my best to be that, until I could no longer keep up with my professional activities and the anxiety I felt. He wasn't happy, and I wasn't happy.

I felt burned out and exhausted from running my own business. I was doing my best to keep up with my professional development, take care of my sons, and attempt to take care of this relationship. I finally decided to close my business. Just as it had been difficult for me to decide to leave my private Ob-Gyn practice, it was also difficult for me to leave my patients at my new practice. I had spent so much of my time, energy, and money to create a new way of taking care of women, and I knew that I was losing the excitement and motivation I initially had when I first started my practice. I traveled back and forth from Canada and D.C. to attend different events and training during the year. After the last event in November, I returned home and collapsed into bed for three days. Everything seemed to be falling apart, and I felt defeated. I decided that this was the time to withdraw from the world. I felt like I didn't have the energy to go on anyway.

WHAT WAS I DOING WRONG?

While Mark tried to be supportive during this time, our relationship was also falling apart. Although we tried to keep things going for the next six months, it was impossible to stay together, nor was it wise or healthy. We didn't see each other much during this time, and I started to reflect deeply on who I was if I wasn't a devoted physician, mother, and lover.

What I finally could see clearly was that while I had shifted some things in my life and created much more space for myself after quitting my job, I was still running many of the same scripts in my head. I was still defining my value and worth by my work and my usefulness to others. I was still using romantic relationships to soothe my dysregulated nervous system. I was always placing the locus of control for my happiness and peace outside of myself. I would idealize the person I was dating, but then soon become irritated and resentful about the things I didn't like about that same person.

Disillusioned and weary, I decided to stop working altogether. I knew I could not continue with things as they were. My strategies to stay safe were not working. Feeling extremely tired and unable to get out of bed some days, I went to see a new functional medicine physician. While I found it challenging to let go of the reins of control, I finally let her suggest and order testing to evaluate my debilitating fatigue and my now increasingly depressed mood. We discovered that despite clean eating and intermittent fasting, I had multiple food sensitivities, low levels of all sex hormones and cortisol, and many nutrient deficiencies. There was also the reactivation of an Epstein-Barr virus, with a very low white blood cell count. It was not surprising because I had remained in a survival mode state even after leaving my conventional medical practice. My mind had stayed in that state even though I had significantly changed my external circumstances and had more freedom and control over my time.

I understood that relying on external conditions for my happiness was neither safe nor wise. Yet, I continued to believe that caretaking and control were the means for me to feel love and worthiness. For my very wounded self, I had to slow down almost entirely to access the ability to return to myself... to stay with myself. In the end, I realized that I left myself behind years ago. I had separated and divorced myself years and years ago. So, how could I live differently?

SLOWING DOWN, LETTING GO, AND FEELING GOOD

I surrendered to everything happening around me, and I slowed my life to what seemed like a near standstill, a crawl. I only did what I wanted to do. March 2020 arrived, and the world shut down with the terrifying pandemic's rise in the United States. My sons were now home with me too, and I felt like I had all that I needed to rest and recover...finally.

I focused on healing my gut health by eliminating all of the foods to which my body was immunologically reactive. I took daily meditative walks to the local rose garden park, and I sat on the same bench every day to be quiet with myself. I took photographs of roses, flowers, trees, the sky, bunnies, and anything else that was beautiful to me. I ate very mindfully and regularly, with a diet full of organic fruits and vegetables, more than I had been feeding myself before. I noticed that I felt more even and steady again. I began to run again and practice improvisational yoga in the park. The return to my love of running and yoga was remarkable, because I had not had the energy to do much in the previous months. Letting go and feeling good was my practice now. That's all.

As I continued to slow down and quiet my mind, I felt less worried about the future. Living in the present, moment-by-moment, I began to have longer and longer glimpses of real joy and genuine love for myself. Committing to self-care and the cultivation of greater equanimity were the keys to my return to true joy, true love, deep inner peace, and feeling vibrantly alive.

THE JOURNEY BACK TO YOURSELF

If any of what I shared with you sounds familiar, then you know that it is not easy to find your way back to knowing your intrinsic high value and worth. You are worthy of great love simply because you are. You are always first in line for your love. Attempting to find that love outside of yourself is not reliable or safe because the only locus of control we have is within ourselves. We do not have any control over what others do or think. Nor do we really want to control what others do or think. Love for yourself attracts love from others. The truth is that only when you love yourself deeply will you find someone who can love you deeply as well. True love for yourself will bring you the happiness and joy you so deserve and desire.

If you are thinking right now that you are not sure how to find your way back to loving and staying with yourself, know that I understand that journey very well. I know that you can find your way to true love. I did, after many years of not knowing how to get there. In the pages ahead, we will discover the path back to loving yourself. You will understand the conditions that are needed to cultivate to find true love. Begin by believing that finding true love is possible!

HOW CAN YOU FIND TRUE LOVE?

"Go back and take care of yourself.
Your body needs you; your feelings need you; your perceptions need you.
The wounded child in you needs you.
Your suffering needs you to acknowledge it.
Go home and be there for all these things.
Practice mindful walking and mindful breathing.
Do everything in mindfulness so you can really be there, so that you can love."

— Thich Nhat Hanh,
True Love: A Practice for Awakening the Heart

You can never find the right answers unless you are asking the right questions. As a physician, I have always been persistently inquisitive. I became more and more curious about the roots of true wellness and inner peace. I completed a two-year fellowship in integrative medicine and then spent another two years studying functional medicine. In the meantime, I completed yoga teacher training and spent countless hours with my Tibetan Buddhist teachers in meditation and receiving teachings. Ever-seeking I am, and always will be. One of the greatest lessons I learned along the way was that finding joy and feeling good first was the key to finding the answers that I had been searching for my whole life. Feeling good first allows your consciousness and perception to expand to attract opportunities that would not have been previously accessible.

In Chapter 7 of *Physician, Care for Thyself*, I tell the story of finding a healer named Hope among the mystical red rock peaks of Sedona, Arizona. Feeling good and letting go allowed me to tune in to myself. Learning to stay with *me* shifted my life onto a new path of being and seeing. I share this excerpt from the book to relate how I started to ask different questions about finding true love.

> "I couldn't understand the right questions to ask until I began working with a healer named Hope. The thing that seemed crazy was how I met Hope. I did not seek her out directly as I had with multiple therapists, psychiatrists, acupuncturists, and other healers. I was simply following my bliss by taking a trip to mystical Sedona, Arizona. It was the first vacation I had taken in years. I met Hope after climbing a steep one-mile hike up to the peaks of Cathedral Rock. Both Hope and I live in New England, about one hour away from one another, so to have our first meeting between the magical formations of Cathedral Rock was genuinely fantastic. After finding ourselves in a part of the rocks that most people don't know about, we talked lightly about how beautiful and breathtaking it was to be

where we were. No personal details of life were exchanged. As I turned to hike back down, Hope looked directly into my eyes and said, "I think you may need my help. You are facing some big decisions." Completely mystified, I blinked back at her and replied, "How did you know?" This was the beginning of my journey with Hope.

Because I had opened myself up to find the real questions I needed to ask, I found Hope, thousands of miles away from home, up high in one of the most mystical places on Earth. I had been asking with my heart, and I was ready to face the questions. The more important lesson to me here was that feeling good and finding bliss first led me to see and find what I needed. This was the opposite of what I had been doing all of my life. I thought that there were multiple checklists and checkboxes to complete before I could feel good. Who knew that I would find answers unexpectedly by feeling good and finding bliss first? And the more we step in the direction of feeling good, the more ease we have in our lives. This is simply the truth.

When I started to work with Hope, I was asking her questions about whether to close my current functional medicine practice. I could clearly and quickly see that I was repeating the same cycles of working, exhaustion, and depression that I had been experiencing in my work as a conventional doctor. This may or may not come as a surprise, because I worked with root causes as a patient of functional medicine and a practitioner. What I soon discovered was that I hadn't yet addressed the real root cause of my exhaustion and depression.

Hope is an energy healer who uses her gifts of intuition to coach and uses energetic tools to uncover further the roots of feeling unwell. What we quickly discovered in our first session together was that I had developed the core belief at the age of six months that meeting the needs of others was more important than meeting my own needs. Not an earth-shattering discovery, right? And yet, it was critically vital to explore the roots of this core belief. The question underneath the question of how to love myself was: *what separated me from that sense of love in the first place?* What created this belief that meeting the needs of others was more important than meeting my own needs? The imprint of this mistaken belief led me to believe that all of the answers lay outside of myself."

As improbable as it may seem that I developed this false belief so early in my young life, I can see how it colored everything that I did in my life. I believed that if I could control my external life and meet the needs of others around me, only then would I be happy and find love. Finding Hope started me on the path to finding true love. Choosing this loving path begins your journey back to you.

THE PATH AHEAD TO FINDING TRUE LOVE

In Chapter 4, we start with the first essential step to finding true love: slowing down. We will discuss how living the increasingly swifter and faster-paced modern life blocks access to your ability to access your self-love. You will learn about living in your limbic system, in survival mode, as you rush through your life to carry out all you feel pressured to get done. Living in survival mode with the soup of survival stress hormones makes it nearly impossible for you to learn a different way to be and live. Slowing down will allow you to see your life with curiosity and learn to respond from the higher areas of your brain, namely the prefrontal cortex. Practicing slowing down to watch your thoughts and feelings will give you the power to shift your beliefs about yourself and reconnect with the life and love you want.

In Chapter 5, we will explore the vital importance of creating mental clarity through the care of your physical body, beginning with your gut health. Did you know that there are direct connections between your gut and your brain? It's called the gut/ brain axis. If your gut is sick with inflammation and cannot digest and absorb nutrients, your brain will also be inflamed and undernourished, along with the rest of your body. You will learn about what harms the gut/ brain axis: sugar, an unbalanced gut microbiome, and a leaky gut. A leaky what? When the gut lining barrier of the small intestine is compromised, not only can we not digest and absorb food properly, we also risk exposing ourselves to harmful microbes, toxins, and undigested food particles that are seen as foreign to our immune system. What results after leaky gut develops will vary and can lead to any type of symptom or illness. You will learn what you can do to heal your gut and gut/ brain axis to keep your overall mental clarity and vibration high. Developing the power to take care of your body and mind will allow you to stay with yourself more consistently.

In Chapter 6, we will take a good look at how we chronically abandon ourselves through our false beliefs, thoughts, feelings, and actions. Using the work of Dr. Margaret Paul and her Inner Bonding process, I will walk you through the six areas where we may be habitually abandoning ourselves. These six major areas are centered around our *emotional, physical, financial, organizational, spiritual,* and *relational* lives. Awareness is the first step to having greater wisdom and living more lovingly and skillfully.

In Chapter 7, we will dive deeply into the challenging

work of learning to stay with yourself. This is an ongoing process that we practice throughout our lives and return to when we inevitably veer off course. You will want to build a framework and process that you can come back to again and again to strengthen those pathways in your brain and body to love yourself directly and unconditionally. You will learn about the importance of being open to learning about the false beliefs that you created to protect yourself and that are no longer serving you. Eventually, you will develop and strengthen a greater understanding and ability to stay with yourself, to love yourself deeply, and to act from the most loving place to care for yourself.

In Chapter 8, we will address the need to become clear about what you want and the importance of defining your boundaries. Defining boundaries is not a straightforward issue for some of us. This is especially true if you were raised in a family where there was no clear delineation between you and your caregivers. After defining boundaries, the next big step is to assert yourself with others to acquaint them with your boundaries. Without defining and keeping boundaries, you will never develop the ability to stay with yourself and love yourself consistently.

We will also discuss defining boundaries before starting to date and be in relationships with partners. Reflecting on and writing out your requirements for relationships will help you to be clear about what you want and don't want in a relationship. We often compromise ourselves when we tolerate those who don't meet our requirements in a relationship. This invariably leads to conflict and dissatisfaction. Your aim is to create a relationship in which you feel inspired, one filled with warmth and ease. Begin with cultivating that same warmth and comfort with and within yourself.

In Chapter 9, we will start to delve into the topic of

dating as a practice of staying with yourself and living with self-love. After sowing the seeds of love and cultivating strong roots of self-love, you can move forward with dating as a practice of becoming comfortable with uncertainty, developing courage and bravery, and seeing where you still need to care for yourself more deeply. The more we move out of our comfort zone, the more we meet endless opportunities to grow and live life more fully and joyfully. Finding another to share in that journey starts with being inspired by who you are! Your inner light will guide you toward meeting people who inspire you and with whom you can explore a deeper connection.

In Chapter 10, I remind you that you are always first in line to receive your love. As we continue to move forward in life, we will often fall back to familiar patterns of beliefs and habits. Often, living what is familiar is more comfortable than having the courage to step out beyond what you know so well. The key to staying in the space of self-love and self-connection is to make room for all that nourishes you and brings you joy. We will return to the cultivation of metacognition through quiet practices such as meditation, yoga, spending time in nature and sunshine, and other ways to allow your body to relax, rest, and be safe. Your self-care practices will be the inner wellspring of your happiness, love, and joy throughout your life.

REMEMBERING WHO YOU ARE

You are beautiful inside and out, worthy of the greatest true love that will never leave you: your love for yourself and who you are. If you are anything like me, there are days when that self-love is nowhere to be found. When your friends or family encourage you to take care of yourself, you may feel too much confusion, frustration, sadness, or anger to love yourself. "I know that, and I just don't know how!" You say to them or yourself. You may not find yourself ready for anything written in this book, and that is OK. You are ready when you are ready.

Know that I've been in that place of habitually abandoning myself, with little access to my deep self-love. I felt like giving up many, many times. Nevertheless, I didn't give up, because I had brief and then more extended glimpses of my joy and love. I became more and more curious about how to stay there and to stay with myself. Staying with the curiosity at first was more straightforward than staying with me. Press on and stay with the idea of finding your true love. One day, you'll find that it's become much easier to stay with yourself, to abandon self-abandonment!

Let's start by taking a few deep breaths with long exhalations to slow down and calm yourself. I am here for you. *You are here for you.*

4

THE FIRST ESSENTIAL STEP TO FINDING TRUE LOVE: SLOW DOWN

*"When everything around me is moving so fast,
I stop and ask,
Is it the world that's busy?
Or is it my mind?"*

— Haemin Sunim,
The Things You Can See Only When You Slow Down

Back when I was in the midst of the madness that is Ob-Gyn residency training, I had just returned from giving birth by an emergency C-section six weeks before to my first son, Ben. It was too soon to be returning to a crazy busy work schedule, while breastfeeding and caring for my newborn baby boy. While life as a new mom was chaotic and beautiful, life as the chief resident on the gynecology surgical service was sometimes pure lunacy.

Wake up at 5 am. Breastfeed Ben after having fed him three hours earlier. Coffee. Shove a bagel into my mouth while getting dressed. Hop into the car at 5:45 am. Arrive on the floor at 6 am — round on ten patients with the team. Write notes on all patients. Review surgical assignments for the rest of the team. Run down to the pre-operative area at 7:15 am to meet my patient, review the procedure, answer questions, reassure the understandably nervous patient and her family, obtain a signed informed consent, smile assuredly that everything was going to go well, and run off to scrub up for the case. Soon to follow is a probably very difficult hysterectomy for this terrified woman whom I just reassured. Scrub. Breathe deeply. Enter the super-bright and clean, sterile operating room. Greet the nurses. Don the gear to operate; gown, double-gloved with size seven Bio gel gloves. The patient rolls into the room. Create calm for everyone in the room — smile under my mask. Perform surgery seamlessly while teaching the junior resident how to do the same. Ouch. Breasts full of milk for Ben. Finish case at 10 am. Run to the call room. Pee. Pump for ten hurried minutes. Hungry. Run to the cafeteria for a quick bite of an energy bar. Shoot! The next case begins in fifteen minutes. Off to pre-op. Shampoo, rinse, and repeat for the next three cases of the day.

WHAT DO YOU MEAN SLOW DOWN? ARE YOU KIDDING ME?

Slow down, you say? I was a new mother, wife, and chief resident in a bustling urban hospital in those days. I never really had time to think until the end of the day when I finally fell into bed. And even then, I couldn't rest and sleep, as my mind ruminated on the surgical cases of the day, how little time I had to spend with my newborn son and my husband, the quality of the breast milk I pumped that day, the next day's cases, losing the baby weight I had gained, and on and on and on.

You likely have your version of living life in a kind of blurred existence of running from one task to another, feeling pressed in by all that you have to do. While there has been much more focus on slowing down with mindfulness practice recently, we generally live in a culture of doing everything more efficiently and more quickly. Go, go, go! Faster and more efficient looks like faster food, smarter phones, Amazon Prime delivery of anything you want right to your front step, electronic everything, speedier internet service, and access to anything at your fingertips, right now. I want it right now. I can have it right now.

Probably more concerning is how your attention is pulled in so many different directions now. If you are a parent, working your job, having young children, and taking care of a house is more than enough responsibility. Tie this to your split attention on your Facebook, Instagram, and Twitter accounts, to the news, to the advertisements on social media targeted explicitly towards your interests, emails, texts, and phone calls. Do you find yourself using your smartphone as your constant source of distraction? All of this is information overload. We were not designed to be taking in all of this into our minds and beings. It's too much. It's truly too much for already overloaded minds and nervous systems.

All of this activity and distraction does not give any of us space to be quiet or to be clear minded about what we truly want in our lives. More and more information and distraction. Less and less ability to focus and to create. All of this keeps our attention focused on our external material reality and our control of that external reality. All of this keeps us in a survival mode state, because if you can't keep your life together somehow, it feels like everything will simply fall apart. You just can't let that happen. You feel as if you are the linchpin that is holding everything together. For busy mothers, this isn't too far from the truth.

Slow down, you say? The suggestion that you slow down seems completely ludicrous and impossible. Yet, the truth is that if you do not choose to slow down, you may never have access to the more profound wisdom within you. If you are not yet in contact with your intrinsic worthiness and love, then you may never find it if you are still feeling hurried and pressed in your life. Why? Because your brain and body perceive that you are in survival mode nearly always. Being anxious, rushed, and worried does not cultivate the conditions for finding the true love you want. You may know this deep down inside, and many days you may wonder, *how can I possibly slow down?* Wondering and having curiosity is the perfect place to start. You can pause for a moment and start right now. You may hold that spark of curiosity in your mind and heart for years before you feel that it's safe for you to slow down. This is your life and whatever you decide is what is right for you in the moment.

WHY IS IT SO HARD TO SLOW DOWN?

How do you create the conditions for slowing down? You can start by understanding some of the basic neurophysiology of what keeps you in a fast-paced, reactive survival mind-state. Starting here can help you understand the vital importance of slowing down.

Have you heard of the limbic system of your brain? The limbic brain houses a structure called the amygdala. The amygdala is activated when we feel threatened or fearful, the *fight-or-flight* response. You've heard that before. The *fight-or-flight* response is adaptive and appropriate when there is real danger present, like when you're driving to avoid an accident or when there is a clear physical threat to your safety or those you love. You want the release of epinephrine and norepinephrine to push blood to your extremities, forcing you either to defend or to run. You want all of the resources of your body to help you to survive the threat. It's a good thing.

And with the rush, rush, rush, and information overload of modern life, you may be chronically living within your limbic system, hijacked by constant reactivity to all you need to deal with regularly. Fortunately, you have higher and more evolved areas of our brain, the frontal lobes, which supply some ability to regulate your reactions, and allow that gap and pause before acting. The prefrontal cortex (PFC) handles the much-needed executive function of self-control, planning, decision-making, and problem-solving. The part of you that can create, grow, and thrive resides in the ability to live in a *top-down* way, with the PFC governing the inputs to the limbic system. You can observe what you are thinking and how you are reacting. This ability to watch and be aware is called *metacognition*, the ability to rise above your thoughts. You develop and cultivate the power to observe your feelings and thoughts before responding.

Yet, the reality of this frantically paced modern life is that you may feel frequent worry and have anxiety about the next thing to do. You worry about what you posted on Facebook and what your friends posted on Facebook. You need to call back the teacher who is calling you again about your child. You are feeling overwhelmed about multiple deadlines at work. You ruminate about the disconnection that you feel with your partner and the sadness you feel about that disconnection. Then, you remember you have to pick up the kids from soccer practice. The thoughts seem endless. What will you make for dinner? When are you going to start exercising again? Why do your pants feel so tight? How do you lose those pounds you've gained over the past year? When can you finally have that glass of Pinot Grigio when the kids are finally in bed and asleep? You cherish any small sliver of time when you can feel a tiny space of relaxation and quiet that may only come with that glass of wine (or a few).

You may or may not see yourself as being in survival mode. And if you have anxiety and worry in your life, you are in some kind of state of survival because you live in some sort of suspended state of concern about the future and the past. Living in the past and the future with your thoughts and emotions limits your ability to be present right here, right now. It limits your ability to think clearly and act from a balanced perspective of what is happening right now.

When you are stressed and worried, the amygdala activates pathways of stress in the hypothalamus in the brain, which then stimulates the release of the stress hormones by the adrenal gland: epinephrine, norepinephrine, and cortisol. These hormones impair the all-important top-down regulation and executive function of the PFC. Memory and ability to regulate your attention are then attenuated and sometimes disabled. You have less control over where you place your attention. The release of these hormones also strengthens the conditioned responses to fear mediated by the limbic system and amygdala. This *bottom-up* mode of living reinforces negative emotions and generally less skillful ways of responding to events outside of your control.

Over time, your habits of mind become more and more ingrained within your being and existence, solidified in what we call your personality, who you are and how you act in the world. The ability to slow down to observe and be aware becomes less accessible as you find yourself sometimes or often in a reactive state. This way of being has become more and more the rule rather than the exception in contemporary life.

These days, we only have to take a brief glimpse of our

country's current political leadership in 2020 to see this in a full-blown and exaggerated way. The seeming unconscious and hurtful reactivity is how things look when operating in a mentally bottom-up way of life: mindless, aggressive, foolish, and low-vibration. This kind of energy feels terrible, terrifying at times, and out of control.

HOW DO YOU BEGIN TO SLOW DOWN?

If you feel like this at times in your own life, know that you have a choice to live differently. You can experience the *top-down* life of living in a higher-vibration state of creation and growth, which allows you to have greater access to healing and remembering who you are and how to love and value yourself.

You are the one who can become conscious of all that is arising in your life, all of the thoughts and emotions. You have sovereignty over how you live your life and when you can begin to lift yourself out of survival mode thinking. *While it may seem like your life is rushing around you, pause to consider whether this starts in your mind that is so busy.* How do you begin to slow down your mind?

Slowing your mind begins with the intention to slow down, having the curiosity about what it might look like to slow down. It starts with understanding that you can never reach the life you truly want to be living without turning down the volume on those things that keep you in a survival mode, bottom-up way of thinking, feeling, and acting.

For me, this process began with leaving my job as an obstetrician/gynecologist. I wrote about this arduous journey in my first book, *Physician, Care for Thyself*. Although I truly loved my patients and much of what I was so privileged to do in the office, the delivery room, and the operating room, my super-busy lifestyle kept me in a chronic state of massive stress. Interestingly, as an Ob-Gyn, I performed in a top-down manner with my PFC, mostly in charge of my emotional responses while working, especially in emergencies. I was well-known for being extremely calm and collected. This took an immense amount of energy. When I returned home, I could still show up reliably and lovingly as a mother, but I didn't have room for much else.

When I finally dared to quit my conventional medicine job in May 2016, the tightly tied knots of my habits of thinking, feeling, and acting began to loosen. Beginning to slow down and reduce the volume of all of the endless inputs to my brain was an excellent start to slowing down. Over the next four years, I began to break the habit of being myself described so powerfully in Joe Dispenza's groundbreaking book, *Breaking the Habit of Being Yourself: How to Lose Your Mind and Create a New One* (Hay House, 2012). Steadily, I began to move from living from a place of fear and anxiety to one of love and clarity. I began to live a life I could never have imagined years before, running from the operating room to the on-call room, pumping milk for Ben between cases, and then back to the operating room again.

I now live a life of love, freedom, and happiness! Do I still bump up against difficulties and challenges? Of course, I do. The difference is that now I can observe them as opportunities for growth and healing. How do you start to slow down and begin to cultivate the skill of metacognition, the ability to pause and reflect, to stay with yourself? We'll explore the necessary conditions to create the life and love you want in the next chapter.

5

ALIGN YOUR BODY AND MIND TO FIND TRUE LOVE

*"Nourishing yourself in a way
that helps you blossom in the direction you want to go is
attainable,
and you are worth the effort."*

— Deborah Day,
Be Happy Now! Become the Active Director of Your Life

Have you heard that all disease begins in the gut? I would further modify this quote from Hippocrates to read, "All dis-ease or *lack of ease* starts in the gut." This assertion may seem unfamiliar or maybe like an overstatement to you right now, but it is true.

Before I understood all that I now know about nutrition, digestion, and food, I used to use food to satisfy hunger and sometimes for enjoyment. Back in the frenetically paced days of Ob-Gyn residency training, I often didn't eat until odd hours of the night, or while running between cases. I distinctly remember running to the cafeteria at Hartford Hospital and heading straight toward a light-heated contraption that held foil-wrapped hamburgers and cheeseburgers alongside grease-stained sleeves of fries. I never had much time to eat, so I'd grab a burger and fries, stop to slap some lettuce, tomato, pickle, and ketchup on the burger, and feel relieved that I had something to eat between the operating room and rushing to see patients in the clinic. Some days, I had a few minutes to sit with my friends to quickly catch up on the latest gossip and news of the day. Most days, I didn't. Many days, I'd eat peanut butter sandwiched between two graham crackers, coupled with Styrofoam cups filled with the worst, diluted, awful "coffee," and that would do it. That was the nourishment for the day.

Then, when I was in private practice, my favorite on-the-go breakfast was a *healthy* turkey sausage with egg white and cheese flatbread sandwich, followed by a Grande Mocha Latte with an extra shot of espresso. Later, I'd have a twenty-ounce Diet Coke to augment my caffeine intake for the day. I still felt so drained and tired by the middle of the morning from seeing so many patients in the office.

Writing that just now was a little painful. Why? I didn't know at the time that every day, I was creating more disease within my body with the low-quality food and drink that I was consuming quickly and mindlessly. Not only was I sleeping irregularly and working long and strenuous hours at the hospital, but I was also poisoning myself with food that isn't food because it doesn't truly nourish the body. The only movement that I had in my life was running from task, to task, to task. Eventually, after years of treating my body and mind this way, I developed worsening depression and anxiety.

Meanwhile, after my divorce, I was on the endless hunt for love. At the time, I didn't realize I was looking for love in all the wrong places. I also didn't know that I would never shift out of my well-worn habits of thoughts, feelings, and actions without physically aligning my body and mind. Without inner alignment, I was never going to discover how to find true love for myself.

Why is this so important? I think we understand that eating well and having a healthy lifestyle, including daily movement and exercise, are essential. And most of us don't know how critical gut health is to brain health and our bodies' overall health. A healthy body and mind are crucial for mental clarity and staying in the best state of mind. Maintaining our gut and brain health supports the ability to remain in that *top-bottom* functioning of the prefrontal cortex discussed in the previous chapter. It gives us a better ability to engage in metacognition, rise above our thoughts, and increase our consciousness and awareness around our thoughts and choices. So let's talk about this all-important concept of the "gut/ brain axis."

THE GUT/ BRAIN AXIS

First, what is the *gut*? The gut includes everything needed to digest and absorb the food that you eat: your mouth and salivary glands, your esophagus and stomach, your small and large intestines, your liver and gallbladder, and your pancreas. Your digestive tract is so wonderfully and beautifully designed to harness the energy and nutrition stored in good, whole foods.

The gut connects to the brain in two primary ways. The first is through the vagus nerve, the primary modulator of the parasympathetic nervous system. The sympathetic nervous system mediates the fight-or-flight activity, while the parasympathetic nervous system is responsible for relaxation to allow us to rest and digest. The vagus nerve sends and receives messages from the lungs, heart, kidneys, and all of the gut organs. So, there is a direct hotline to and from the brain to the gut through the vagus nerve.

The second way the gut connects to the brain is by signaling through hormones and neurotransmitters. When the hormones and neurotransmitters of stress are chronically activated, gut health can become compromised. Over an extended period, the ability to digest and absorb food can no longer work as it was designed. Compromised digestion leads to malnutrition and then every disease possible. As Hippocrates asserted, "All disease begins in the gut."

Start with the concept that gut inflammation leads to brain inflammation. There is now copious research proving that brain inflammation is directly correlated with illnesses such as Alzheimer's and Parkinson's, seizures, ADHD, depression, anxiety, and any brain-related disease. How is food related to the compromise of brain function? Let's look at the influences of sugar consumption, an imbalanced gut microbiome, and a leaky gut. For a much more comprehensive view on gut and brain health, read David Perlmutter's book *Brain Maker: The Power of Gut Microbes to Heal and Protect Your Brain – for Life* (Little, Brown, and Company, 2015).

WHAT AFFECTS THE GUT/ BRAIN AXIS?

Too Much Sugar

Sugar is a common addiction in modern life. Cookies, candy, milk chocolate, peanut M&M's, and mocha lattes. What's not to love? Sugar is added to so many foods to enhance flavor and keep you coming back to the same yummy foods over and over again. Refined sugar and the inability to metabolize that sugar is responsible for so much destruction and chaos in the body. Elevated serum levels of glucose increase inflammation and contribute to damaging tissues, including the brain.

When we eat sugar, glucose levels increase temporarily in the bloodstream, along with the hormone insulin. Insulin's job is to bring glucose into the cell for normal cellular metabolism and energy storage within cells. When insulin successfully binds with its receptor on the cell surface, glucose receptors increase on the cell surface to take in the circulating glucose to maintain normal blood sugar levels. However, when the body is overloaded with sugar, insulin resistance can develop, and the cellular uptake of glucose is compromised. What happens to that extra glucose in the blood? It begins to attach itself inappropriately to functioning proteins and fats, a process called glycation. Have you ever had a blood test called Hemoglobin A1C? Your doctor may order this test if there is concern about prediabetes or diabetes. Hemoglobin A1C is a glycated part of the red blood cell. An elevated level tells us that you have persistently elevated sugar levels and probable insulin resistance.

Glucose attached to other proteins and fats produces extremely harmful molecules called advanced glycation end products (AGEs). AGEs can also be found in high amounts in meat (especially in red meat), fried, and highly processed foods. AGEs contribute to premature aging, atherosclerosis and heart disease, diabetes, kidney disease, and Alzheimer's disease. The relationship with poor sugar control is so strong with Alzheimer's that researchers are now calling Alzheimer's disease "type 3 diabetes." Stop to think about that. We often believe that we are helpless against aging, disease, and dementia. Reducing or eliminating sugar intake significantly reduces your risk for premature aging and so many illnesses. *Begin to be curious about your sugar intake.*

Consider how you might start to shift your relationship to sugar. Not easy, I know. Maintaining optimal blood sugar control is critically important to maintaining your brain health and overall wellness.

An Unbalanced Gut Microbiome

You have likely heard about the importance of maintaining a healthy gut microbiome for your overall health. You may even be taking a probiotic because you have had issues with your digestive health. As you know, the gut microbiome is composed of trillions of bacteria and other microorganisms and their genetic material and are now understood to be critical for maintaining and controlling our wellness and susceptibility to illness. Did you know that our gut microbiome accounts for two percent of our body weight? If a person weighs one hundred and fifty pounds, that's three pounds of microorganisms within that body!

When in balance, the gut microbiome plays a primary role in our immune system by protecting against infection and inflammation and supporting optimal digestion. It also produces Vitamin B12, thiamine, riboflavin, and Vitamin K. The gut microbiome also directly supports brain health by making beneficial brain chemicals like BDNF and GABA.

BDNF (brain-derived neurotrophic factor) is involved with the growth of new nerve cells and the protection of existing nerve cells. BDNF levels increase with aerobic exercise and the consumption of omega-3 fatty acids, and its production is affected by the health of the gut microbiome. Decreased BDNF levels are associated with Alzheimer's, seizures, depression, schizophrenia, OCD, and dementia.

GABA (gamma-aminobutyric acid) is also crucial to supporting optimal brain function. GABA is the primary neurotransmitter that sends calming messages to your brain, so that you can think and feel better. Alcohol and medications such as Xanax and Valium (both benzodiazepines) increase GABA activity, which is why people sometimes rely on them heavily for relaxation. Consider that part of why people need these substances to relax is related to their disrupted gut microbiome.

For so many reasons, restoring and maintaining your gut microbial balance is critical for brain health and the ability to stay calm and reflect. Remember, top-down functioning from the PFC to the amygdala is what we want to strengthen and support, so that you can start and continue to raise the vibration of your thoughts and actions.

Leaky Gut

The third relationship between food and the compromise of brain function to examine is leaky gut. What is leaky gut? When talking about leaky gut, we are referring to the lining of the small intestine. After the stomach initially processes and digests food, it empties into the small intestine to digest and absorb nutrients. The small intestine also serves as a barrier between the outside world and our bodies' inside world. Housing the gut microbiome, it is also a vital organ of immunity and protection.

Leaky gut occurs when the tight junctions between the cells of the small intestine break down. The lining is only a single-cell layer thick. When the barrier is compromised, harmful pathogenic bacteria and other microbes, toxins, and undigested food particles can enter the bloodstream to wreak havoc. The absorption of nutrients is compromised, and the bloodstream and body are continuously invaded through this broken small intestinal barrier. Because of the resulting state of relative malnutrition and inflammation, a leaky gut can lead to any symptom or disease manifestation.

Leaky gut is associated with autoimmunity: rheumatoid arthritis, Crohn's disease, ulcerative colitis, and Hashimoto's thyroiditis. Leaky gut leads to food allergies and sensitivities, depression, and anxiety. A leaky gut can also lead to a breakdown of the highly protective blood-brain barrier, leaving the brain vulnerable to infection, inflammation, and toxins. *Yes, a leaky gut can lead to a leaky brain.*

What Leads to the Breakdown of the Gut Barrier and Leaky Gut?

- Excessive mental and emotional stress.
- A poor diet, including excessive consumption of sugar, alcohol, processed foods, gluten, dairy, and GMO foods.
- Exposure to toxins such as pesticides, and overuse of antibiotics, aspirin, and NSAIDs like ibuprofen.
- An imbalanced gut microbiome.

In short, a poor diet, the overconsumption of sugar, an imbalanced gut microbiome, and leaky gut all contribute to compromised communication within your gut/ brain axis. While I completely understand that learning about all of this may contribute to your feelings of overwhelm, know that you have so much power to restore the health of your gut and brain!

5 STEPS TO HEAL YOUR GUT (THE 5 RS)

Remove What Causes Ongoing Inflammation in the Gut.

Start with an elimination diet to identify food sensitivities, by removing the most inflammatory and commonly triggering foods, such as gluten, dairy, soy, sugar, and eggs.

Although IgG food sensitivity testing can be useful, an elimination diet is therapeutic and diagnostic, and a required step in healing the gut.

Remove other common causes of inflammation, such as infections (identified through detailed DNA-based stool testing), toxins and medication, and stress. Eat an organic whole foods diet rich with fruits and vegetables.

Replace What the Gut Needs for Optimal Digestion.

- Take digestive enzymes, liver, and gallbladder support.
- Increase stomach acid production through supplementation.
- Use digestive bitters to stimulate stomach acid and bile production and release of digestive enzymes from the pancreas.
- Stimulate of the "rest and digest" aspect of the nervous system (parasympathetic versus the "flight or fight" sympathetic nervous system) via the vagus nerve through the practice of yoga, meditation, singing, slow deep breathing, laughing, and cultivating genuine connection with others.
- Slow down – chew more and enjoy meals and snacks.

Restore the Balance of Healthy Gut Bacteria with Probiotics and Prebiotics, Either through Food or Supplementation.

Admittedly, this is not necessarily the most straightforward recommendation. Which probiotic? What strains? How many billions of colony-forming units? Most probiotic supplements have Lactobacillus and Bifidobacterium strains and can help many people who lack those strains. Consider soil-based, spore-forming probiotics that can survive the stomach mostly intact and can work on many levels to improve gut and overall health. Eat fermented foods such as sauerkraut, kimchi, kefir, tempeh, and miso. Eat prebiotic foods to feed beneficial bacteria: fiber and prebiotic foods such as raw garlic, chicory root, Jerusalem artichokes, bananas, dandelion greens, and jicama.

Repair the Gut with the Nutrients It Needs to Heal and Function Properly.

- Collagen and L-glutamine, both found in bone broth
- Zinc, fish oil, Vitamins A, C, and E
- Demulcent and soothing herbs, such as deglycyrrhizinated licorice (DGL), aloe vera, marshmallow, and slippery elm

Rebalance Your Mind, Body, and Spirit to Rebuild the Foundation for Health and Wellness.

Ultimately, we must address the lack of balance and relaxation we so often have in our lives, leading to poor gut health and chronic disease. We can do all of that is recommended for optimizing gut health, and we may still find ourselves struggling again with the same issues, or worse, not having much response at all. Being quiet and learning to relax is, in the end, the most balancing and healing tool that we all have within us.

NOURISH YOURSELF SO YOU CAN BLOSSOM!

Some of these gut-healing practices you can do on your own. Start an elimination diet focusing on increasing vegetable and fruit intake. Take digestive support and probiotics. Explore relaxation practices. If you have significant issues with digestion, energy, and mood, I strongly recommend consulting with a functional medicine practitioner. You can benefit immensely from a thorough evaluation of your symptoms coupled with functional medicine testing to evaluate your gut health and nutritional status.

Taking care of your gut health to sufficiently nourish your body and brain is another first important step toward aligning yourself with your love. Restoring the health of the gut/ brain axis will provide greater mental clarity and energy. You will feel so much better with significantly increased ability to reflect and know what loving actions you want to take for yourself in every waking moment.

same false beliefs are what caused me to abandon myself over and over again.

You can do the most potent inner work when you are open to learning about the wounded parts of yourself that created those false beliefs. When you uncover those beliefs and what led to those beliefs, you can begin to make your way back to staying with yourself always, to abandoning self-abandonment. In this way, you are taking full responsibility for taking care of yourself. When you take back that responsibility, you then can finally feel loved, peaceful, and safe.

Psychotherapist Dr. Margaret Paul outlines six significant areas of self-abandonment in her best-selling book, *The Inner Bonding Workbook: Six Steps to Healing Yourself and Connecting with Your Divine Guidance* (Reveal Press, 2019). Because I think it is a practical framework to view how we can abandon ourselves, I use it here to show the many ways in which we have difficulty staying with ourselves. These six major areas center around our *emotional, physical, financial, organizational, spiritual,* and *relational* lives. There are no superficial or straightforward fixes for any of these. In the end, remembering and returning to a grounded sense of your own love and care will be the first step toward staying with yourself consistently. Sometimes, though, getting some of these external conditions organized can feel very satisfying, and may motivate you toward even more significant and remarkable shifts in your precious life.

HOW WE ABANDON OURSELVES EMOTIONALLY

When my kindergarten teacher caught me running around the room when I was five, I felt not only guilt about what I had done, but also deep shame. I had already carried around ideas that there was something different and broken about me, and this event served to solidify that belief for me at the young age of five. I launched into a life of constant self-judgment and looking to others for approval and definition of my self-worth. Because I happened to be a smart kid, it was almost effortless for me to use academic achievement and perfectionism to identify myself as worthy of approval and love. And feeling shame is a form of control and a way of ignoring how you feel, a method of self-abandonment.

The false belief behind shaming and self-judgment is that *if you can simply change and improve yourself enough*, you won't be subject to disapproval and rejection. You believe that you can control how others see you by working as hard as you can to gain their acceptance and approval. Sound familiar? The truth is that you don't have any control over how others feel and behave toward you. You alone are responsible for how you feel, and this is a good thing. You can reclaim sovereignty over yourself and your feelings.

Another primary method of emotional self-abandonment is the distraction with whatever addictive behavior you use in your life to avoid feeling what you are feeling. Many people use drinking alcohol, abusing recreational drugs, smoking cigarettes, endlessly checking email and social media posts, excessively exercising, working excessively, taking care of others, binge-watching TV and movies, et cetera. No judgment about any of that because we all have our preferred ways of taking a break from what we are feeling. However, the more we distract ourselves, the more we stay separated from ourselves and our feelings.

During the widely viewed TED Talk entitled "Everything You Know about Addiction is Wrong," British journalist Johann Hari famously asserted that *the opposite of addiction is connection*. In this context, he was referring to a lack of feeling of connection to others. I agree with this wholeheartedly. To truly feel connected to others, you must fully connect to yourself. You must learn to stay with yourself.

The path to emotionally staying with yourself is not easy because it can be incredibly challenging to let go of all of the false beliefs that allowed you to survive your childhood. This kind of work requires the willingness to look at those false beliefs and a skilled psychotherapist's guidance, as well as the support of people who love you unconditionally.

HOW WE ABANDON OURSELVES PHYSICALLY

We can mistreat ourselves physically with how we do not care mindfully for ourselves with food, movement, and sleep. How we nourish or do not nourish ourselves with food is an issue for many of us. Are you feeding yourself a clean, healthy, whole food diet that keeps your body running in a high-vibration state? Are you eating too much or too little to avoid feeling painful feelings?

Are you sitting too much, especially in front of a screen? Are you not moving your body in the ways that feel good to you: walking outside, jogging/running, dancing, yoga, et cetera? Are you driven to over-exercise several times a day to distract yourself or to perfect your appearance?

Are you getting enough quality sleep every night? Are you staying up too late? Or are you waking up multiple times during the night? Are you listening to your body's signals that you need more rest?

As discussed in earlier chapters, giving loving attention to your physical body will allow you greater access to energy and mental clarity. You will have increased ability to pause and respond mindfully to the events around you.

HOW WE ABANDON OURSELVES FINANCIALLY

How we may abandon ourselves financially is very broad. Do you spend addictively, spending too much on things that you don't need, and incurring debt? You may be very rigid about spending money or try to control how others spend their money. You may work too much or too little. You may have excessive anxiety about money, even when you have more than enough money. You may take care of others financially when it is their responsibility to do so. On the other hand, you may be overly dependent on others, or ignore your financial situation altogether. If this is a specific issue for you, find support for yourself to get yourself on track financially. You will feel so much better when you do.

HOW WE ABANDON OURSELVES ORGANIZATIONALLY

While some of us naturally know how to keep our lives organized, some don't seem to manage time and space very well. Are you on time for appointments? Do you pay your bills on time? Do you keep your home and office spaces organized and uncluttered? These may seem like unimportant topics to address, but disorganization in your physical reality does manifest itself in your emotional and mental existence. Marie Kondo's famous book, *The Life-Changing Magic of Tidying Up: The Japanese Art of Decluttering and Organizing* (Ten Speed Press, 2014), can be a great starting point on your way to supporting yourself.

HOW WE ABANDON OURSELVES SPIRITUALLY

We can abandon ourselves spiritually when we don't create the space and time to be quiet and connect with whatever we consider to be our spiritual guidance or spiritual community. If you don't believe in outer spiritual guidance, tune into the need to be quiet with your inner guidance or intuition. This involves strengthening your higher functioning prefrontal cortex and metacognition, as described in Chapter 4. Slowing and being quiet is necessary to tune in to what you need to stay present for yourself, to abandon self-abandonment. We will explore meditation and mindfulness practices more in Chapter 10.

HOW WE ABANDON OURSELVES RELATIONALLY

We will explore this in greater detail in the following chapter, in which you will learn about setting clear boundaries with others. Start with the good news that our closest relationships are the best opportunities for learning and growth – if we're open to that! Why? Because our wounding can be continually bumping up against their wounding, which can often trigger strong negative emotions. Ever experience that?

Because we all need to feel seen, understood, and loved, we will do whatever it takes to be seen, understood, and loved. And the truth is that we first need to see, understand, and love ourselves unconditionally to know and feel true love. Only then can we show up genuinely as one who wants to learn, grow, and share that love with others.

When we are raised in an environment where we don't attach securely to our parents or primary caregivers, we spend a great deal of time and energy seeking love, approval, validation, and a basic sense of worth from those around us. Children who are securely attached to their caregivers feel safe and protected, and when separated from them, know that they will return. Unfortunately, children often do not develop secure attachments to their parents or caregivers, and that becomes a lifelong struggle to feel safe and secure. A deep fear of abandonment and rejection arises, and the boundary between self and other becomes blurred. Whose needs are more important?

Our most important relationships are with our parents, children, partner, close relatives and friends, work colleagues and bosses, and professionals, such as your doctor or therapist. For me, pleasing other people had always been more important than meeting my own needs throughout my life. I felt terrified of losing their approval and care, so I would attempt to control situations and people rather than focus on loving myself and doing what was best for me. I became very anxious when waiting with bated breath to see whether I would get the response that I wanted. I consistently ceded control over my feelings to other people.

What does the attempt to control others look like? It may look like anger, blame, defensiveness, compliance, resistance, and withdrawal. My favorites were compliance and withdrawal. I would do whatever was asked of me, harbor resentment and anger, and then withdraw. I perfected the art of acting sullen and bereft because I believed that I could influence the way others behaved toward me. Acting like a brat is not a skillful way to build connection and trust with others. Yet, because this strategy seemed to work intermittently, I often believed this was the only way to relate to others in difficult situations.

Another common form of control is to act as a caretaker or a taker. As a caretaker, you take responsibility for taking care of any or all the other person's needs, most often that of your partner or parent. If you are a taker, you relinquish responsibility for taking care of your own needs to the caretaker. Either way, neither person is taking responsibility for their own needs and feelings. Anger, resentment, and dissatisfaction are inevitable with a caretaker/taker relationship.

For me, I frequently played the caretaker role in romantic relationships because I believed that if I made myself somehow indispensable to the other, then I would never be left or abandoned. In this way, I became entirely dependent on the other for my sense of worth and self. After all, if I could provide for all his needs, wouldn't that be proof enough of my worth? Ooof, that is so painful to write and read because I have fortunately moved forward from this belief. This is part of the root cause of why I could not find a healthy relationship. I was abandoning myself for the other and attempting to control how the other felt about me and the relationship.

What does a healthy relationship dynamic look like? Both people enter the relationship taking full responsibility for loving and filling themselves with love. Both want to share their love and desire the other to feel happy, free, and fulfilled. Both want the highest good of themselves and the other. Both remain open to learning about the other, and conflict becomes an opportunity to strengthen and grow the relationship. Both feel safe to share their feelings and needs openly. In this loving system, intimacy grows and flourishes. Sounds great, huh? It all starts with staying with yourself first, abandoning your chronic self-abandonment.

As with breaking any habit, breaking the habit of abandoning yourself will be a challenging and lifelong practice. In the next chapter, we will explore what first steps you can take to learn to stay with yourself. After slowing down and taking care of your mind and body, you will be well-prepared for this life-changing work of finding true love. This work was what allowed me to connect with my inner joy and love, at long last!

LEARNING TO HOW TO FIND TRUE LOVE

*"Do I prefer to grow up and relate to life directly,
or do I choose to live and die in fear?"*

— Pema Chödrön,
The Places That Scare You: A Guide to Fearlessness in Difficult Times

After spending months with a therapist named Theresa, I felt the need to address, once again, the longstanding depression and anxiety I had struggled with since college. Theresa was the fifth or sixth psychotherapist I had worked with during the previous nineteen years. I had begun to feel that medication and therapy were a futile attempt to make myself feel better. During my second year in medical school, I had finally consulted with a psychiatrist for the first time and began a long series of different medication trials to treat depression. Some medications seemed to help for a little while, but then invariably stopped helping.

I had been relentlessly pushing myself very hard in medical school, in residency, and now in my private Ob-Gyn practice, getting little sleep and often feeling very unsupported in whatever relationship I was in the time. The only sources of relief seemed to come from the time I spent with my children, my time with whatever romantic partner I had at the time, and my time with patients in my office and at the hospital. Connection with others and helping others were the only sources of relief I seemed to have from the sometimes debilitating depression and anxiety.

One day, Theresa asked me to imagine my three-year-old self. I closed my eyes and could see myself in a dark blue dress with little pink flowers, and my straight black hair pulled back into two pigtails. I was smiling with a fluorescent pink Frisbee in one hand. This image of myself came to mind because it's one of the few photographs I have of myself from when I was very young.

"Can you see yourself as a three-year-old, Jessie?" Theresa asked. I nodded, and she asked me to open my eyes.

"Look across at the chair in front of you and pretend that pillow is you when you were three. What do you see, and what do you feel?" She asked me.

I glanced over at the red, linen throw pillow I imagined my young self, sitting there swinging her feet back and forth with eyes looking downward. The edges of her lips turned low in a sad frown. Young Jessie looked irretrievably downcast and miserable.

Hot, wet tears flowed down my cheeks. "She seems to be very sad," I replied slowly.

"And what do you feel right now? What do you want to say to her?"

What do I feel, and what do I want to say to her? What

was Theresa asking me to do? Initially, I felt incredibly confused by the questions, and then I began to seethe with burning anger and rage.

"I hate her. I hate her so much. I feel like I want to hurt her and hit her. Why is she so sad? Why? Why?" I started to sob violently and thrust my face into my hands.

"Can you hold her right now? I think she needs you to hold her." I looked up, glared at Theresa, and spat out, "And why would I want to do that? She's horrible and broken and doesn't deserve to be held or loved!"

She pressed me further. "Would you ever say that about your sons, Ben or David?

At that point, I couldn't handle anything more and ended the session with Theresa. I understood what she was trying to accomplish with me, but I didn't understand how to get there.

In the end, it wasn't medication, psychotherapy, romantic relationships, my performance at work, or even my beautiful children who were going to help me find my way back to myself and learn how to stay with myself. I continued to believe that pushing myself harder and harder to be perfect at work and home would ultimately prove my value, and that my sense of worth and love was only to be found in a partner or at work. If I held tightly to those false beliefs, I would never have a genuine opportunity to remember my intrinsic worthiness and my love for myself. *I needed to look directly at my patterns and false beliefs that had interfered with intimacy with myself and others.*

When I finally made the choice to slow down, I did. I quit the job I had created and then closed my functional medicine practice to stop working at any job altogether. I gifted myself the time and space to reckon with all of the false beliefs I had created to survive when I was very young. I now had the mental bandwidth and time to take care of my body and mind with all the knowledge that I had gathered from my integrative and functional medicine training. I slowed down, leaned into my discomfort, and aligned my body and mind through clean eating and daily movement practices.

Gradually, step-by-step, I found that I now had access to my love for that sad three-year-old sitting across from me. I have since taken her into my arms, and now cradle her with the warmth and love that I give to my own children.

"Do you love me now?" she asks.

Now I can reply in every moment, *"Yes, Dear Jessie, I love you very much. I will never leave you. I am here for you always, to protect and cherish you."*

WHAT'S GOING ON INSIDE THAT PRECIOUS HEAD OF YOURS?

As a functional medicine doctor, I have learned that there are always multiple causes and conditions for the symptoms of illness. The road back to our bodies' beautiful innate balance requires looking at those root causes and conditions to create the roadmap back to feeling good and whole again. The same is true of the search for love. As I related in my story of moving from extreme self-loathing back to genuine self-love, I needed to slow down, restore health and balance of my body and mind, and observe what I was feeling and doing to myself over and over again. I believed that the solutions to my problems lay outside of myself, so I desperately attempted to control my external reality to meet my needs.

I realized that I was continually abandoning myself with my self-judgment, numbing my feelings, and making others responsible for how I felt. It was no wonder that I was suffering from what seemed like recurrent treatment-resistant depression and anxiety! I repeatedly Googled the term, *treatment-resistant depression* because I could not figure out how to feel better. The more I struggled with it, the more broken I felt.

Of course, many therapists and friends would repeatedly advise being gentle with myself, to take care of myself, and I didn't understand how to do that. Theresa, the very well-meaning therapist, attempted to direct love toward the hurt inner child. Little did she or I know that I was continually trying to destroy her and myself. *I didn't know how to stay with myself because doing that would mean dismantling all of the false beliefs and methods of control I had created to survive.* As a sensitive child growing up in a very confusing family environment, I constructed and did whatever I needed to survive. And considering dismantling that was terrifying.

I do believe that working with skilled psychotherapists, functional medicine practitioners, and other healers is necessary when a person is experiencing major depression, severe anxiety, or any other mood difficulty that interferes with your ability to heal. Working with trained trauma specialists is essential for those of us with a significant history of trauma. I needed more work with intuitive energy healers, a psychotherapist well-trained in Internal Family Systems work (https://ifs-institute.com), and a hypnotherapist, in order to continue to open access to my inner knowledge and self-love. Peter Levine's book, *Healing Trauma* (Sounds True, 2008) and Resmaa Menakem's book, *My Grandmother's Hands* (Central Recovery Press, 2017), are excellent resources to support the resolution of trauma energy stuck in the body. There are lots of layers and so many knots to untie! It is so worth doing the hard work to get to the other shore of true love and happiness.

Despite the terror of leaving behind my old false beliefs and habits, I knew that I had to continue to search for answers. I genuinely wanted to grow up and take full responsibility for my life and my choices. I did not want to live and die in fear. So, I pressed on. Eventually, after slowing down and restoring the balance of my body, I found the answers I had been looking for all of my life. Because there is always more to discover, life simply gets better and better with each layer uncovered! This is the beautiful truth of the journey back to loving yourself fully.

LEAN INTO THE DISCOMFORT AND TAKE RESPONSIBILITY FOR YOUR FEELINGS

Admittedly, this isn't straightforward advice or guidance. Because I know it isn't easy, I first wrote about the importance of slowing down and raising your energetic vibration by taking care of your physical body, primarily focusing on your gut health. I know that doing these two things makes this process much easier because you can create the conditions that allow you to pause, feel calm, and observe with curiosity what you are feeling. You will sometimes fall back into familiar patterns and reactivity. From time to time, I certainly do, and I've noticed that I spend increasingly less time there and much more time in an observing and curious space. What a relief!

The truth is that the only thing we truly have any control over is how we handle our thoughts and feelings when they arise. Cultivating the conditions that allow you to remain as much as possible in that top-down control from the PFC to the limbic system is vitally important. As discussed in Chapter 4, having the skill to observe first and then respond with mindfulness gives you the power to move in the world with more ease and comfort. You won't be banging up repeatedly against the reactivity of others or reacting to something as a threat when it isn't one. You can maintain your inner ground and peace, and you can avoid unintentionally hurting other people. You alone are responsible for your feelings, and this is a good thing. You can reclaim sovereignty over yourself and your feelings.

Developing a quiet practice of meditation and mindfulness is helpful and essential to becoming familiar with your habitual thoughts and beliefs. You may decide to take up a formal meditation practice with a trusted spiritual teacher. You can take a structured course like Mindfulness-Based Stress Reduction (MBSR), an eight-week, evidence-based program designed to strengthen your resilience if you struggle with depression, anxiety, chronic pain, and ongoing stressors. One of my favorite and most accessible books on beginning meditation is *Mindfulness for Beginners: Reclaiming the Present Moment and Your Life* (Sounds True, 2006) by Jon Kabat-Zinn, Ph.D. Or, you can simply sit or lie quietly for a few minutes to start.

OPEN YOUR MIND AND HEART TO LEARN ABOUT YOUR WOUNDED SELF AND ITS FALSE BELIEFS

There can be many blocks and obstacles to realizing the felt experience of loving yourself. I know this from my many failed attempts to sit with and examine my wounded self. I also understand that you may not feel ready for this level of work. Start where you are. *Being curious is an excellent place to begin.* Be curious about what is possible for you!

Who is this wounded self? When you were very young, you were taking in everything as new and fresh. You were born worthy of great love, and you remain worthy of great love. However, what if you didn't grow up with consistent nourishment, encouragement, affection, and love from your parents or caregivers? What if instead you were exposed to neglect, emotional, or physical abuse at times? We all have a fundamental need to connect with and attach to people who love us and whom we love. When that young and developing connection is compromised or distorted, you feel pain, suffering, and hurt. If not addressed or recognized at the time, this wounding lives in your being and body.

To survive and make any sense of this experience of repeated trauma, you developed certain beliefs to protect yourself. You needed to deal with a confusing reality that was damaging to your young and sensitive nervous system and brain. When you feel threatened or hurt in any way, you will act to defend and protect yourself. Whether jumping out of the road to avoid an oncoming truck or hiding in your room to avoid further conflict with your parent, you will find ways to deal with the threat or pain. Your young self often couldn't defend or protect from external circumstances, so you developed strategies and beliefs to deal with the reality of your life. In this process, you may have left yourself behind in order to avoid feeling the deep pain of being hurt by the people you loved.

Then, for the rest of your life, your view of yourself and others is colored by beliefs that no longer serve to protect you. You continue to limit and hurt yourself by holding on so tightly to the beliefs that you needed to survive as a child.

What are some of the false beliefs that you still carry around with you? Many of these beliefs may center around not being *enough*: not smart enough, not attractive enough, not desirable enough, not supported enough, not loved enough, not recognized or understood enough, not stable enough, or not perfect enough. Or, perhaps you think, *if only the people and circumstances around you were better*: your partner, your job, your parents, your friends, your children, your house or apartment, your car, or your finances. Whatever they are, these false beliefs separate you from your love and sovereignty over yourself. In the end, you are the one making the choices, and you can choose to believe differently, feel differently, and live differently.

The first step is to be open to learning about yourself, to observe the one who has all of these false beliefs. Observe with gentleness, kindness, and no judgment. After all, you created false beliefs to deal with all-too-overwhelming reality when you were younger. To be gentle, kind, and non-judgmental toward yourself may be incredibly difficult at first because these false beliefs are accompanied by a lack of acceptance of who you are. And all of you, all parts of you, are worthy of loving, kindness, and compassion.

Observe without judgment. Observe that those false beliefs were created with the intent to protect yourself and control others and circumstances. Interestingly, while it seems that these beliefs serve you, they don't. False beliefs keep you in a state of bondage to external events and the words and actions of others.

For me to be gentle with myself took many years of hard work because, after all, I had used so much of my time and energy to construct an identity that required perfection to survive. Unrealistic expectations ruled my world, and of course, I could never achieve perfection to please everyone around me and satisfy my wounded self. With diligence and determination, I finally reached a place of self-acceptance, gentleness, and love. You can get there, too.

CHOOSE TO STAY WITH YOURSELF

When you feel anxious, sad, angry, frustrated, agitated, jealous, or any other uncomfortable feeling, ask yourself what your feelings are telling you. Enter a dialogue with yourself whenever you can. Sometimes, this is impossible, such as when we are entirely flooded with the emotions of the moment. Either now or after the intense emotions have passed, ask yourself:

What am I continually telling myself that creates feelings

of sadness, anxiety, anger, shame, jealousy, hurt, unworthiness, hopelessness, and loneliness, et cetera? What am I trying to control or avoid? Can I stay with myself and not flee into my preferred ways of coping?

A recurrent theme in my life was feeling anxious when I felt that things were not going as I wanted in a romantic relationship. The relationship became a stand-in for any sort of safety or stability that I had been looking for as a child. If I felt that my partner was not responding as I wanted, I would begin to feel anxious. For example, if I sent a good morning text to my partner and then didn't hear from him as I usually did, I would begin to worry. *Did I do something wrong? Is he OK? Why isn't he sending a good morning text back? Maybe he isn't really that into me.* I would hurl myself into a world of unrest and apprehension. In the past, I would only feel some relief after hearing an explanation from him.

I have now learned to pause when I begin to recognize the all-too-familiar feeling of anxiety. What am I telling myself about this situation and myself? Is it true? What do I know? What am I trying to control or avoid? What am I feeling in my body? In this case, I was trying to define myself, and my worth, by another's actions. I wanted him to act in specific ways to reassure myself that I was worthy of love. Eventually, when I practiced staying with myself, this anxiety no longer arose as often, because I didn't need to rely on another to define my worthiness of love. Practice with yourself. You may simply begin, as I did, by saying out loud, "Stay with yourself."

DETERMINE THE MOST LOVING ACTION TOWARD YOURSELF

After you can dialogue with yourself about what you are feeling, you can then consider the most-loving next action for yourself. Too often, when we're feeling uncomfortable, we look for something to distract us. These are the ways that we abandon ourselves emotionally, as we discussed in the previous chapter. Again, no judgment about doing this. We all do it and will continue to do it until we have built more steady and reliable habits for staying with ourselves.

A concrete way to stay with yourself and the uncomfortable feelings is to journal or do some other activity to express yourself: paint, dance, or color – whatever you can do to be with yourself and your feelings. Journaling can be so helpful for observing what you are feeling. When you write down what you're feeling and what is happening around you, often you gain insight into what to do next. Sometimes, writing it down is in itself therapeutic.

The most-helpful next thing is always to do something to care for yourself in some way. In the beginning, reaching out to a trusted friend to talk can be very helpful. Eventually, you want to be able to soothe yourself with self-care: a warm bath with sea salt and lavender, taking a nature walk, practicing restorative or yin yoga, or meditation. *Cradle yourself with your own love.* Feel what it feels like to receive your love.

Over time, when you can stay with yourself more consistently and reliably, you will begin to trust your ability to choose yourself first. You no longer rely on the approval and actions of others to determine how you feel about yourself. You say "No, to people, places, and things that harm you in any way.

The most beautiful thing is that you begin to reclaim you and your life. You choose what pleases you. You enjoy your time with yourself. If you have divorced or broken up from a long-term relationship, you reclaim your physical space, time, and energy. For example, that room that was your partner's office can become a wellness space for you to do whatever you like!

A crucial part of staying with yourself is remaining clear about your boundaries and not allowing others to cross them. This is all part of remembering who you are and reclaiming your life as you want to live it. In the next chapter, we'll look more closely at this much-discussed issue of maintaining personal boundaries and how you can be crystal-clear about what you need and want.

8

DEFINING THE BOUNDARIES OF TRUE LOVE

"Daring to set boundaries is about having the courage to love ourselves,
even when we risk disappointing others."

— Brené Brown

"Do you like dogs?" He asked during one of our initial phone conversations before meeting for the first and only time. I had noted on his Match.com profile that he had multiple images of himself hugging and nuzzling his Pembroke Welsh Corgi, alongside others with the faces of his children scratched out. It should have been a firm "no" for me from the beginning, based on these photos alone. I decided to talk to him anyway, since he was a kind-of-cute real estate broker who lived in my town. I had attempted a few longer-distance relationships in the past and wanted to date someone who lived closer to where I lived.

This need for proximity seemed to be an essential requirement at the moment.

"Uh. Dogs are OK. I don't like dogs who are yappy and jump all over me," I replied slowly, again thinking that this conversation needed to end now.

"Oh! You're not a dog person! What else should I know about you?"

He was hilarious and engaging on the phone, so I decided to meet him despite multiple red flags, including a particular text conversation. I told him that I wanted to go very slowly, especially with physical involvement. He then asked me if it was because I didn't like sex. Again, everything should have ended right there. I went to meet him for dinner anyway because it seemed harmless.

After a dinner, during which I spoke very little, we were standing at our cars when suddenly he gave me a tight hug, and I could feel the gross squishiness of his entire body. Then, he abruptly smushed his lips on mine and then quickly moved away from my face.

"What was that?" I asked, scowling.

"I just kissed you, and I can do so much more," he replied, with the stupidest grin on his face. He moved toward me, and I pushed him away. He moved toward me again and told me how sexy he thought I was and what he wanted to do to me. I backed away, quickly hopped into my car, and sped away. WTF?

I can count at least twenty times when I needed to say, "No," to that entire scenario. I fully admit that I allowed it to go much further on other dates when I didn't want it to. Many of us have been there before. While I hate to admit it, I have given in to men in the past when I didn't want to. I had been afraid that if I didn't, the guy would feel disappointed, angry, or wouldn't love me anymore. These are clear physical and emotional boundary violations that I allowed. Could the guys have been more sensitive to what was going on with me? Yeah, but it's not their responsibility to take care of me or my feelings. I have the choice of whether to say, "No," or not. And saying "yes" when I want to say "no" is abandoning myself and my needs.

HOW DO WE DEFINE OUR BOUNDARIES?

Discussions around personal boundaries are more common these days, as people explore maintaining healthy boundaries with those in their lives at home, work, and play. Boundaries can be defined as the limits we set when interacting with other people. They indicate what we find acceptable and unacceptable in their behavior towards us. The ability to know our boundaries comes from a healthy sense of self-worth. You value yourself in a way that is not contingent on other people or their feelings toward you.

And then this is the difficulty, the very confusing and challenging rub. You need to have a healthy sense of self-worth to begin to understand boundaries and how to respect them for yourself. Knowing that boundaries can actually exist can be very demanding for those who have experienced significant trauma in our families of origin. As children, we relied entirely on our parents or caregivers for unconditional care and love. The birthright of every human being is to be loved simply for being worthy of love.

Unfortunately, some parents do not have the tools to care for, love, and consistently protect their children. Boundaries can be violated physically, emotionally, and intellectually. Repeated violations become a pattern of abuse that blur the lines between the child and parent. Sometimes the roles are switched and the child is forced to care for the parent physically and emotionally in exchange for some sense of belonging, love, and protection. In this setting, it is almost impossible for a child to develop any coherent understanding of appropriate boundaries.

What can then follow is the endless search for unconditional love elsewhere, especially in romantic relationships or having sex with multiple partners without regard to safety or self-respect. Rather than having an intrinsic sense of worth cultivated by loving and considerate parents or other caregivers, you may feel that your value can only be defined externally through others' approval and acceptance. Maintaining personal boundaries becomes nearly impossible because your very sense of who you are is inextricably tied to what others think and do.

HOW TO START TO DEFINE BOUNDARIES TO PROTECT YOURSELF

"Protect yourself, Jessie! You're so sensitive, and you need to set boundaries and keep them." I heard this advice repeatedly from friends, therapists, spiritual teachers, and even my divorce attorney! Yet, I still had a great deal of difficulty understanding what that meant or how I was supposed to do it at all. I understood that when I made particular decisions to gain approval or avoid rejection, I often felt a sinking feeling inside. I realized later that this was a distinct and reliable body-sensed signal that I chose to ignore.

Begin to notice when you feel discomfort, anxiety, anger, resentment, or frustration with someone when asked to do something that you may not want to do. These feelings may indicate that you are allowing a personal limit to be crossed. You may want to start to write down these feelings when you notice something, like when your boss asks you to stay late to complete another project, when you need to get home to your family. Or when a new date kisses you unexpectedly and wants more.

Defining your boundaries can sometimes be confusing. Your definitions will also change and evolve as you grow and change. Tuning into how you feel about different situations will give you invaluable guidance about your boundaries. If you are just beginning to be familiar with this practice, keep a journal of what you feel when something happens that you think could be a boundary violation for you. In the beginning, checking in with people whom you trust for further consideration can be beneficial. In the end, though, it is your inner knowledge that will guide you best.

BE BRAVE AND ASSERTIVE WITH PROTECTING YOURSELF

The first step is to become familiar with what your boundaries are. The next step is also very challenging, and for most of us, it will take a lifetime of practice. You cannot assume that anyone knows your boundaries, so you will need to let people know. Again, your sense of self-worth is tied intimately to your comfort with asserting yourself. Your practice of staying with yourself and discovering your self-love will help with this immensely over time.

Start with smaller, more manageable requests like asking the server to split the bill among all parties at the table when dining out. Why is this a boundary issue? If you only want to pay your part of the bill, it is best to split the check. Or, if you notice that the cashier has overcharged you, ask for the amount to be corrected. These things may or may not be comfortable for you to do. The point is to practice more with less important things. Then, at some point, you'll be better equipped to assert yourself during more challenging situations.

You may believe that asserting yourself will be perceived as selfish, mean, or rude. Remember that you have no control over how things are perceived. What is more important is that you practice valuing yourself, your needs, and your feelings over others' thoughts and opinions. I know that this kind of practice isn't at all easy if you have spent a lifetime believing that your needs were not as important as others' needs. You abandon yourself when you continue to allow your boundaries to be crossed.

What if you voice yourself firmly, clearly, and repeatedly, and the other person still does not respect your boundaries? Then, you have the choice to take a break from that relationship. In the case of strangers or acquaintances, you can end the conversation and break off the connection. Remind yourself that you matter most to yourself. You are no longer willing to leave yourself behind to avoid rejection or hold onto love. Over time, these kinds of interactions will happen less often. You will choose to have only supportive and understanding relationships in your life.

HOW TO BUILD TRUST WITH OTHERS AND YOURSELF

In any relationship, platonic or romantic, the basic requirements of great connection are chemistry, compatibility, and communication. How do you determine whether you are making choices based on old patterns and habits of attraction? Suppose you have made choices to be with people with whom you believed you had great chemistry, compatibility, and communication. Were you staying with yourself and listening to your inner guidance? Were you faithful to and honest with yourself?

Because I didn't grow up with clear boundaries with my parents, I developed a great deal of confusion around self-love and self-worth. I understand now that my choice of romantic partners was often informed by a set of false beliefs about myself and others. I had to construct a new paradigm for deciding who to date and whether to continue to pursue a relationship with that person. Sometimes, it was very obvious to me when things weren't working out. Still, most of the time, I stayed longer than was healthy for me. How do you make better and more aligned decisions for yourself while dating? How do you begin to feel safe and trust the one you are getting to know, and how do you continue to cultivate self-trust?

"THE ANATOMY OF TRUST"

Courageous and wise, Brené Brown is a social research professor and master storyteller. She became hugely popular after her 2010 TEDxHouston talk on vulnerability went viral. She has spent more than twenty years researching courage, vulnerability, shame, and empathy. In 2015, she gave another groundbreaking talk, "The Anatomy of Trust," which aired on Oprah's podcast, *SuperSoul Conversations*. If you haven't heard it, look it up and listen to it, because it will shake your world. During this talk, she uses the acronym BRAVING to describe what creates trust. Boundaries, Reliability, Accountability, Vault (confidentiality), Integrity, Non-Judgment, and Generosity are the aspects of the anatomy of trust that she teaches. People build trust with each other in the small, everyday moments of connection.

The mnemonic BRAVING serves as a potent tool for determining whether you can trust another person with your story and love. More importantly, it provides a well-grounded framework for gently evaluating trust in yourself. When you know what your boundaries are, can you trust yourself to maintain them? Can you stay aligned with your truth? Can you remain non-judgmental and generous with yourself? My wish for you is that you can! Listen to the talk and learn to fill yourself up with your trust and love.

DEFINING BOUNDARIES IN RELATIONSHIPS

After realizing that I wasn't consistently listening to myself when dating or in other relationships, I began to examine in earnest my boundaries and why I found it challenging to maintain them at times. I found this valuable exercise in *The Boundaries Program*, an online course taught by life coach Bryan Reeve. It's so simple and can be so revelatory!

To better understand your boundaries in relationships, he asks you to define your requirements and requests within your romantic relationship. This practice can be used with any relationship in your life. A requirement is non-negotiable for you, something you must have in a relationship to feel comfortable and happy. A request is something you may prefer, but do not require within a relationship.

When I started dating again, I wanted to be clear about what I needed and wanted. I have been perplexed about clear boundaries in the past. I had not thought too hard about what was negotiable and non-negotiable for me in a romantic relationship. I soon realized that I needed to be applying this rubric from the very beginning when choosing to date anyone! It's not always easy. We all want to believe that when we are in love, we can accept everything about each other. This is a dangerous belief that can lead to resentment, conflict, exhaustion, and ultimately the end of that relationship.

My current requirement list looks like this:

- He must take care of himself physically, emotionally, mentally, and spiritually.

- He must respect my physical, emotional, intellectual, and spiritual boundaries.
- I feel a deep emotional and sexual connection with him.
- We are monogamous.
- We fully honor the no's of the other.
- We have and maintain open, honest, and transparent communication.
- He cherishes me and my feelings.
- He is intellectually and emotionally my equal.
- He doesn't own pets. (Kidding! Not kidding.)

While the list may seem earth-shatteringly demanding, actually writing it out made it so clear that I had not been honoring myself or my boundaries. This list revealed how I had been abandoning myself and my needs repeatedly in dating and long-term relationships. As I move forward in my life, I refine this list more and more. Do this for yourself now – as soon as you can – and discover what is essential for you in a romantic relationship. For other relationships in your life, you may have different requirements. Evaluate those requirements and boundaries as well. A necessary act of self-love is to know and honor what you need and want.

PRACTICE TRUE LOVE WHILE DATING

*"Daring greatly means the courage to be vulnerable.
It means to show up and be seen.
To ask for what you need."*

— Brené Brown

With my newly defined boundaries and relationship requirements, I returned to my preferred online dating site to see whether I might attract a relationship of inspiration! Despite having recently experienced that awful, awful date with the Corgi-hugging, squishy, bump-into-my-face kissing guy, I had decided that dating would continue to be great practice with becoming comfortable with the truth of uncertainty, impermanence, and detachment from outcomes. Yes, I can be a little intense and spiritually nerdy. I had been listening diligently to talks by Brené Brown and Pema Chödrön during my morning walks, so why not practice by daring greatly and dating greatly?

I don't like online dating sites. Who does? Trying to find someone attractive, interesting, kind, and intelligent requires a certain amount of hunting. One day, inspired by Brené and Pema, I happened upon a very handsome and attractive man. He impressed me with photos of his perfect handstand on a paddleboard and a witty profile comparing online dating to Zillow. Funny! And there was an unexpected bonus: he lived in my town. Handsome, hand-standing, humorous, and hometown. Perfect. I love alliteration and alignment! I dashed off a quick and friendly note, and soon afterward, I had a reply from him that was light and cheerful, and he invited me to meet for coffee the next day. We both ordered iced decaf oat milk lattes (I love iced decaf oat milk lattes!). I noticed that he tipped the barista twenty percent. I liked that.

We walked and talked effortlessly, and decided to sit comfortably, cross-legged, on a stone wall next to the labyrinth in the town center. And for the next ninety minutes, we laughed, smiled, and shared; nothing too serious. We talked about our love for our children, our work and play life, yoga, hiking, and our dreams for the future. We both wanted to travel cross-country and tour the United States, and to travel as much as we could worldwide. He wanted to take a sabbatical from his job as an attorney to explore writing a book and expanding his love for photography, possibly into a business. I shared that I was discovering what I wanted to do with my life after quitting my job as an Ob-Gyn.

I switched careers to practice integrative and functional medicine, and I had written a book! The time passed quickly, and I had this distinct feeling of safety and ease with this person. We parted with warm smiles. It was an excellent start and a date that was quite different from my date with the squishy guy. I felt inspired and happy and looked forward to seeing him again soon.

DARING GREATLY AND DATING GREATLY

Once you have set out to discover true love for yourself, and to learn how to remain present for yourself, you may be ready to share that love with another person. You are now equipped with better tools to practice trusting yourself, maintaining your boundaries, and listening to your inner guidance and intuition. The ideal path is to rediscover and embrace your love for yourself first, and then be inspired to share that love with another person.

Living life can either be one big arena of practice, from moment to moment, or it can be an experience of repeated cycles of struggle and pain. Choose the first path, and you will find yourself growing and expanding in ways that you've never imagined! This may sound a bit "Pollyanna," but it is true. Choose the courageous path of slowing down and taking care of yourself. Become open to learning how you sometimes keep yourself stuck. Remain aware of yourself and your needs. Choose the most loving action for yourself. Use every experience, whether it feels good or bad, to inform how to move forward with greater wisdom and ease.

The more we practice moving out of our comfort zone, the more we encounter opportunities to grow and live life more fully and joyfully. What better option than to practice through dating? While we often risk feeling hurt by dating and being in relationships, it is through these experiences that we expand and grow. Facing our most wounded and vulnerable places directly, with limitless compassion and gentleness, will strengthen us beyond belief.

Dating does not need to be the ultimate search for *the one*. It can be simply going on adventures to meet new and interesting people. I continued with dating in order to practice and to engage with people with whom I could learn and grow.

I will never claim to be an expert on dating and relationships. I share what I've learned from getting back up and brushing myself off after many dating experiences. You will learn something from each experience, which will help you refine what you want, and become more explicit about boundaries and staying with yourself during the process of sifting and sorting through your experiences. Ready to start?

START FROM A PLACE OF INSPIRATION

You cannot truly love another unless you have learned to fully love yourself. This is a crucial part of what is presented in this book. When you place the locus of control for love outside of yourself, you are in an unstable and insecure place. The only love you can rely on unconditionally is that love which you have for yourself.

Everyone in the world is dealing with their wounds and, hopefully, their healing process. Everyone is responsible for their awakening and remembering who they are. When you choose to embark on the journey of remembering who you are and your magnificent love for yourself, you will want to find another who is doing the same. Happy people attract happy people!

Become inspired by who you are, what you love, and the warmth of your love and kindness. If you have children, tap into that unconditional love you have for your children, that love that inspires you to be playful and joyful. Feel good first. Be happy first. Then make choices and act from that place of high-vibration and creativity.

Imagine what that relationship of inspiration feels and looks like. During the pandemic's initial days in 2020, I started to walk every day to the local municipal rose garden and listen to the *Modern Love* podcast. This podcast is based on the popular weekly column in *The New York Times* and is narrated by notable celebrities. The stories center around love, loss, and redemption. Some of the stories and accompanying narration will move you to tears and inspire you to find your own modern love story. Two of my all-time favorites are "When Your Greatest Love Is a Friendship" by Victor Lodato, and "The Race Grows Sweeter" by Eve Pell. I can listen to these two stories over and over again because they are utterly gorgeous and moving.

When I listen to the stories, I connect with my ever-loving heart. I tune in clearly to what true love is for me: kind, warm, fun, smart, funny, shared, considerate, intelligent, wise, appreciative, together, comfortable, easy, tender, connected, open, safe, creative, awe-inspiring, loving, sexy, being, flowing, exhilarating, exciting, new, old, reliable, trustworthy, generous, surprising, erotic, vital, growing, enjoying, savoring, delicious, gorgeous, grateful, full, abundant, happy, joyful, blissful, alive, expanding, discovering, friendly, graceful, strong, abiding, faithful, curious, heart-centered, understanding, and compassionate. Read this paragraph out loud to yourself. Then, be inspired to get going on your own list!

If you feel unable to do this, you may not be ready to date. Ideally, you want to be happy and feeling your best before attempting to meet the partner of your dreams. Otherwise, like me, you'll meet the *almost* person; never the person with whom you can continue to grow and play. Take the time you need to remember who you are and your love for yourself.

SHINE YOUR LIGHT

The reality of dating these days is that much of the meeting occurs through online dating sites. If you can, though, go to places where people are doing what you love to do: yoga, running, hiking, birdwatching, playing tennis, or whatever it is that you enjoy! It can be an excellent start to finding someone with shared interests and mindsets.

The first thing to do is choose which site you want to use, if you haven't had any online dating experience. You'll need to try a few of these sites. Or, you can ask friends who have used different sites which ones they prefer. All of these sites have different algorithms for matching you with different people. I'm not going to endorse one over the other except to say that some are less annoying than others. Be aware that all of them use technology to keep you endlessly checking and choosing. How to best use online dating? Slow down, be healthy in body and mind, stay with yourself and your self-love, maintain boundaries, and know what you want.

WRITING YOUR PROFILE

Take the inspiration from reflecting on the way you want to feel in the relationship of your dreams. Talk about what you love. Be sincere and genuine. Your profile needs to show who you are. Present yourself as your beautiful and glowing self. This will be easy after you've done your inner work, as we've discussed in previous chapters. If you don't feel this way yet, that's OK! I didn't feel this way for years. I first had to learn to stay with myself. Traveling my personal path to healing and freedom eventually allowed me to meet this need. This journey never ends, and that means that things can only get better and better!

As an example, this was my latest profile posting:

YOU CAN FIND TRUE LOVE

"I am a bright, active, and ever-inquisitive woman looking for an equally engaging, active, intelligent, mindful, and kind man to enjoy life with!

I am blessed with two genuinely amazing sons. They are kind, independent, super-smart, and loving human beings. It's so easy and fun to be their mom!

Maintaining a healthy mind, body, and spirit are necessary aspects of every day of my life. I am looking for the same in my partner. I love to cook, dance, walk, run, hike, and practice yoga barefoot in the grass. I take photographs of beauty in nature. I love being anywhere outside, especially near water of any kind. One of my favorite places on Earth is Bailey Island, Maine, along the majestic, craggy coast. Breathtaking. Awe-inspiring.

I've always been and continue to be passionate about my work as a physician. Now, I've created a life in which I can work the hours I want while pursuing things I've always wanted to do, like write books and speak publicly. While I value stability and security as much as most, I also require excitement, novelty, and creativity. I like living on the edge of discovery, learning what lies next over the horizon. I love what happens when you set a clear intention to create. The world can open up to you in ways that you've never imagined!"

What am I communicating with what I wrote?

- Who I am: Am I bright, active, curious, creative, and free?
- What do I value and want: a healthy mind, body, and spirit; engaging, active, intelligent, mindful, and kind. Novelty and excitement!
- What I enjoy doing and what inspires me.

The upbeat tone of what I wrote is intended to attract someone with the same energy and enthusiasm. You should write what reflects who you are, what you value and want, what you enjoy doing, what inspires you, and what you want to attract. Shine your light brightly!

POSTING PHOTOS

Your photos also need to reflect your light. Smile! Look into the camera directly. Post photos doing what you love to do. Show yourself having fun. Again, the photographs should reflect who you are, not what you think others want to see. This will be easier when you are more comfortable with staying with yourself and loving everything about who you are right now.

CHOOSING WITH WHOM YOU WANT TO COMMUNICATE AND MEET

Honestly, this is a practice of just doing it, trial and error, because getting to know someone online is completely unnatural! Given that, there is some guidance that I want to share with you.

When you are sifting and sorting through the hundreds of online profiles, keep in mind the list of requirements you have made. Have that list sitting with you as you look through the photos and click on different profile listings. Stay with yourself. It's easy to get lost in examining pictures of perspective dates and reading monotonous descriptions of what they may enjoy, want, and desire. If you feel inspired by someone, reach out to them in a lighthearted way, perhaps referring to something you enjoyed reading in their profile. For example, since I enjoy yoga and paddle boarding, I was incredibly fascinated with the photo of my date doing a perfect handstand on a paddleboard. He posted that photograph to inspire those who were impressed to reach out to him, and I did!

Many will reach out to you to connect. Again, be discerning. Most will not say too much. You may get greetings such as "Hi, Beautiful!" or "Nice pics!" I ignore those kinds of messages. I expect someone to make an effort to engage with me meaningfully. For me, meaningful engagement is an essential first step. Notice how the message makes you feel. Do you feel interested, inspired, or excited after reading the content and looking at the profile? Or, do you feel put off, bored, or irritated? Respond only to messages from people with profiles that genuinely resonate with you. Stay with yourself.

As for messaging, texting, and talking before meeting, I prefer not to communicate too much before meeting my date in person. Have a phone conversation or two first to see whether you have any interest in meeting in person. My experience has been that sometimes communicating too much before meeting creates a false sense of closeness and trust. Trust is something that is created and earned over time. And remember that your physical safety always needs to be considered in this modern world of online communication. Ask for the person's last name and do some research online before agreeing to meet anyone. This is the advantage of modern-day technology! It may feel a little weird to be doing that kind of research, but it is necessary these days to confirm a person's real identity.

CREATING A RELATIONSHIP OF INSPIRATION!

Ken Page is a skillful dating coach and psychotherapist who hosts a weekly podcast called *Deeper Dating*. Take a listen if you want some constructive advice on dating and relationships. He often talks about an attraction of inspiration versus an attraction of deprivation.

Unfortunately, many of us are very familiar with the attraction of deprivation. These are the relationships that started with the people who *almost* provide all that you need. However, over time, they trigger anxiety, a fear of abandonment, and an ongoing sense of inadequacy. It feels good some of the time. You stay because you believe that feeling good some of the time is worth sometimes feeling anxious and inadequate. How many times have you experienced this or watched your friends do this?

On the other hand, an attraction of inspiration is firmly grounded in what you want and need. According to Page, an attraction of inspiration is filled with warmth and ease. The attraction is fueled by a sense of well-being, joy, safety, and goodness. The relationship of inspiration unfolds slowly over time and continues to get better and better. Doesn't that sound better? By staying with yourself, loving yourself fully, and honoring your boundaries and requirements, you will eventually find yourself in a soul-satisfying relationship of inspiration. Then, not only will you have true love for yourself, you will have the joy of sharing your love with the partner of your dreams!

10

PRACTICE TRUE LOVE WITH YOURSELF EVERY DAY

*"When you recover or discover something that nourishes your soul and brings joy,
care enough about yourself to make room for it in your life."*

— Jean Shinoda Bolen

"Yo, I'll tell you what I want, what I really, really want. So, tell me what you want, what you really, really want. If you wanna be my lover, you gotta get with my friends. Make it last forever; friendship never ends…"

Do you have songs that you love so much that you can play them over and over again, dance like a wild woman, and feel great? The 1996 Spice Girls smash hit "Wannabe" is one of many of my favorites to blast on the Bose speaker in my kitchen, to completely let myself loose in movement and bliss. And if my sons happen to walk in, laugh at their dear mom, and join in, then it's that much sweeter! Dancing anywhere has always been a way of tapping into the part of me that is wild and free, and it nourishes me deeply.

What is that you really want? We've spent nine chapters encouraging you to remember who you are and to rediscover your true lifelong love: you. Once you find your true love again, how do you support a lifelong romance with yourself? The reality of living this life with all its external stressors and pressures is that it is all too easy to fall back into patterns of self-abandonment. Habits are sometimes incredibly challenging to break, even when we know changing those habits is what we really, really want. What will be so critical will be to develop daily self-care practices that you come to find to be indispensable for your well-being.

We all set goals to eat well or exercise regularly. We can be convinced that these practices are essential to restore and maintain health. We can intellectually understand how vital these things are to our well-being. We can even start or sustain a new habit and feel great about what we're doing, only to fall back into old habits when some event or stressor interrupts that newly found routine.

This can be especially true for those of us who are more sensitive to others' energy. Call us highly sensitive or empaths, it can be challenging to discern what is my energy or that of another. I love that I can feel so strongly the joy that others are feeling, but at the same time, I can feel their sorrow equally as profoundly. My inclination is then to put aside my own needs to take care of theirs. Sometimes this is appropriate, such as when the need is grave or very urgent. However, if you chronically consider others' needs more important than your own, you will need tools to help support doing what you want and need. Making self-care a daily practice that you enjoy and value will require making close friends with ways to keep aligned with your wants and needs. After all, if you want to be my lover, you have got to get with my friends! Who are these daily friends who can support loving and staying with yourself?

In Chapter 5, we discussed the vital importance of restoring and maintaining gut health for mental clarity and overall physical health. By caring for the gut/ brain axis, you have a better ability to access that top-down control of the prefrontal cortex to the limbic system. You have greater access to metacognition, the skill of observing our thoughts and reactions. What other practices or *friends* support your ability to stay in a high-vibration state that allows you to stay connected to yourself and your wisdom?

MAINTAIN CONNECTION WITH YOUR FRIENDS AND FAMILY

Create precious space and time to spend with your family and friends. When you start a new relationship, be careful not to neglect your family and friends. The newest person in your life should not suddenly become the most important person in your life, especially after only a few weeks or months of knowing each other. Choose carefully with whom you spend time. If you find yourself drained after being with certain people, limit your time with them until you find more bandwidth and energy. Do only what brings you joy in your time with others! A clear practice of maintaining boundaries and staying with yourself will keep you in a relaxed and aligned state of mind and heart.

MAINTAINING A CONNECTION WITH THE OUTDOORS AND NATURE

Maintaining a connection with nature is the easiest way to find relaxation and ease in your life. Walk out your door and take a stroll. Gaze at the blue sky. Bask in the warmth of sunlight. Appreciate the flowers in the park or your neighbor's garden. I love running my fingers through fresh lavender buds to take in the heavenly and soothing fragrance.

Ground yourself by walking barefoot in the grass, dirt, or sand at the beach. Lie down in your backyard and stare at the sky. Have direct contact with the Earth, and you will find calm almost immediately. If you don't want to take off your shoes, or if it's too cold to go barefoot, find a giant tree to lean against or sit at the base of. Pick or buy flowers with colors and smells that delight you. Buy houseplants to care for and water. Collect stones, rocks, and crystals to place around your home.

When you wake up in the morning, pause to take in the sunlight and the sounds of birds chirping. Open your window and feel the fresh air on your face. One of my favorite things to do is sit on my front step and watch the sunrise over the rooftops of my neighbors' homes. So peaceful and comfortable.

MINDFUL MOVEMENT

Move your body. You've heard that sitting has become the new smoking. We need to move our bodies to strengthen our muscles and increase blood circulation to all parts of our bodies. Movement increases our breathing capacity and keeps our connective tissues and bones strong and flexible. It also signals the mobilization of stored energy for fuel, to use that fuel for repair and growth rather than store it as fat. Walk, run, practice yoga, or play tennis; do whatever you love to do. The important thing is to find something that you enjoy and will return to day after day. With practices like yin or gentle yoga, tai-chi, or qi-gong, you will relax more deeply and find a space of complete calm in your day.

I love running through the friendly streets of my neighborhood; I always end up at the Elizabeth Park, the oldest municipal rose garden in the United States. With my body warm and loose, I take off my running shoes and stretch barefoot in the softest grassy spot I can find. Downward dog is an incredibly grounding pose and great for strengthening your arms, shoulders, and core. It's also an excellent means of lengthening the usually tight glutes, hamstrings and calves. Lately, I've started a push-up practice, after which I glide myself back into child's pose and plant my face into the grass. I release all of my worries and tension into the Earth. Letting go and feeling good. I usually feel pretty blissed out after this morning practice! Because I love it so much, there is no need to convince myself to get out there. I crave getting out there to run and stretch. Find what brings you joy, and you will benefit from movement, relaxation, and feeling good.

MEDITATION

One of my patients repeatedly told me that she knew that meditation was necessary for finding her inner calm, but that she sucked at it. I always laughed when she said that and asked what she meant. She answered, "Dr. Wei, I can't calm my mind. I don't ever reach that nirvana state that people talk about. I just suck at meditation!" I understood what she was saying. For some, the mention of meditation or mindfulness practice invites resistance and frank disdain. For a few others, engaging in meditation practice without proper guidance can be overly activating, if a person has a significant trauma history.

For most of us, though, an established practice of daily meditation is a time to slow down and to become familiar with our minds and their fluctuations. In his book, *Mindful-*

ness for Beginners (Sound True, 2006) Jon Kabat-Zinn provides this wisdom about beginning meditation practice:

"It is very important as a beginner that you understand right from the start that meditation is about befriending your thinking, about holding it gently in awareness, no matter what is on your mind in a particular moment. It is not about shutting off your thoughts and changing them in any way."

Making friends with your thinking is what meditation is about! Jon Kabat-Zinn Ph.D, is the developer of MBSR, or Mindfulness-Based Stress Reduction. This eight-week course can be a gentle introduction to the skill of quiet practice and greater access to the inner ground and calm that we all have inside of us.

There are hundreds of smartphone apps that you can use to help with finding a few minutes during the day to pause. I like the app that allows me to set the amount of time I want to meditate with a choice of chimes and background music/sounds. There are also thousands of guided meditations of any length that you can use if you are not yet ready for silent meditation practice. I also appreciate that you are connected to thousands of other people meditating with this timer. You have the option of greeting people who have been meditating with you or joining groups with similar interests. The point is, there are many resources available to help you develop a meditation practice. Start with one minute and work up to at least fifteen minutes a day, ideally both at the start and end of your day. The benefits are lasting and powerful and may shift your life in ways that you could never imagine. Meditation is the quintessential practice of staying with yourself.

MAKE ROOM FOR ALL THAT NOURISHES YOUR SOUL AND BRINGS JOY

These are some practical and helpful tools to equip yourself, to nourish your soul, and to bring joy to your heart. When it seems as if everything is falling down around you, your daily practices will increase your ability to face life's challenges with a grace and calm that you may never have experienced before! And it is a moment-to-moment practice. Some days will be easier than others. Pay attention to how much longer you can stay in a coherent flow state as you stay with yourself with your self-care and love.

11

STILL NOT SURE YOU CAN FIND TRUE LOVE?

"The real difficulty is to overcome how you think about yourself."

— Maya Angelou

Once again, I found myself curled up in a ball on the rose-colored carpet of my bedroom. Sobbing violently and rocking myself back and forth. My mother repeatedly banging on the door after I had raced upstairs to escape the chaotic yelling and screaming. I don't even remember what we had been arguing about that time. I never remembered what we argued about because we argued so much. I always wished there had been someone to hold me, to tell me that everything was going to be OK. But there never was.

Shoving my fingers into my ears, I continued to rock back and forth. There were no red ruby slippers on my feet to click my heels together to take me back home. *There's no place like home. There's no place like home.* There certainly wasn't any place like this home, a home life filled with parents continually fighting and the chronic feeling that I could never do anything quite right. There were so many more unspeakable hurts and harm that my young nervous system was never meant to handle. Suffice it say that I experienced recurrent and repetitive trauma as a child and adolescent in this home.

So of course, I needed relief, calm, and quiet. I was determined to find it at all costs and to build a different home life so that when I did click my sparkly, ruby red heels, I would find myself in a home filled with hugs, love, and happiness. I would prove my self-worth repeatedly with academic achievements, going to college, graduate school, medical school, and completing a grueling medical residency training program, and so on. I tried to find love over and over again, with two failed marriages and countless long-term relationships.

I gave birth to two amazing sons. I vowed they would never suffer as I did, with the debilitating emotional impact of growing up not feeling at all safe. I nourished them with hugs, love, attention, and understanding. But I did not do the same for myself. I abandoned myself over and over again in attempting to control how others would feel about me. Little did I know that I needed to come home to myself to find the love that I had been searching for throughout my whole life.

WHAT HOLDS YOU BACK FROM COMING HOME TO YOURSELF?

This Kind of Work Sounds Too Hard

If you have read to this point and think that this all sounds too hard, I understand completely. The journey to untying all of the tightly tied knots of your habits and thinking that have seemed to serve you for so long can often be prolonged and arduous. After all, you created those beliefs and habits to protect yourself from pain and suffering. Why would you want to slow down to look at any of it in the first place? Why would you choose to feel your feelings of pain? No thank you! Or maybe you feel like you can't relate to what I'm saying. You believe that things are going well enough, and even if you have to deal with some anxiety and worry along the way, you're willing to pay that price.

I admit that I have had all of those thoughts so many times along the way. I felt so much resentment that my path seemed to be more challenging than that of other people. Of course, I don't know anything about any other person's path. I do know that when I continued to move forward with small steps; invariably, new opportunities, friends, guides, and teachers would appear to help me. The key was to *keep moving forward* and never to give up altogether. Sure, there were plenty of days spent curled up in bed with the covers and pillows blocking the light of day. Then, I would emerge and start again from where I left off. Again, and again. As I discovered pockets of newfound joy and love, I would remember that I could feel and enjoy those moments. I always knew that the painful moments would pass, and I could feel entirely different in the next moment. That is the beauty of impermanence and change!

So, yes, this is a challenging path – no doubt about it. And if I can do it, you can too!

I Still Believe That If Only...

For the longest time, I believed if only I found the right guy and the right relationship, everything would be perfect in my world. I spent so much time with the *almost* guys. I believed that if he could be more attentive and available, then I would feel loved. If only he knew how wonderful I was, then I would feel accepted. If he could recognize how much I did for him, then I would feel indispensable and important to him. Then, we could live happily ever after, right?

Maybe you make sure that your body and appearance are perfect. Or you believe that if you lost a few pounds or if your nose was a little smaller, it would be easier to find that guy who loves the way you look. After all, isn't it all about physical attraction?

We believe these things because we observe that they seem to work for other people. We wonder, *why can't it work for me?* The truth is, we never know what's going on with other people. I believe the happiest couples are two people who fully love themselves and then share that love. Other couples fit together well enough, tolerating conflict, to live for the days when things seem right. Whatever the case, you will always need to love yourself, whether you choose to be single or in a relationship. People come and go from your life. It is only you who is with you always. So obvious, and yet we often forget that loving yourself is the romance of a lifetime, and so worthy of your precious care and attention.

THE COST OF NOT ABANDONING SELF-ABANDONMENT

The high cost of not abandoning self-abandonment is that you will never live the life you want to live. Believing that if only the other person would change is often the primary way that we relinquish responsibility for our feelings, our sovereignty over our own life.

When I was married the second time around, my ex-husband and I visited a couple's therapist weekly for a year and a half. During almost every session, I would end up sobbing (not curled up in a ball on the carpet, but close!) with the therapist, asking him to hand me a tissue. He would sit with his arms and legs crossed and insist he had done his therapeutic *work*. He would argue that I was the one who had all the issues to fix. While I agreed that I had much personal work to do with my history of depression and trauma, I also felt alone in this journey of making this marriage work. I felt as if he had a brick and mortared a wall around his heart, and he wasn't ever going to let me in.

The truth is that I chose to be with someone who had never let me into his heart. I was so familiar with not being seen and understood that I chose it again. Maybe I decided to marry him to attempt to fix this dynamic that I grew up with during my childhood. Even though I was willing to take some responsibility for my part in the dynamic, we blamed each other for our marriage problems. And because I couldn't tolerate any of it, I left, believing that being with someone else would solve all my problems.

In Chapter 2, you heard about the rest of my relationship saga, with repeated attempts at finding love. After my last breakup, I knew that I had to shift something significant about living my life. *Repeated cycles of the same result and suffering will only repeat if you don't address the actual underlying problem.* After I slowed down and opened myself to learning about my feelings and my responsibility for staying with myself, I finally began to experience the light of my love. I had to overcome how I thought about myself, discovering a beautiful life and love waiting there for me all along.

THE LIFE AND LOVE THAT IS WAITING FOR YOU

Yes, the path to rediscovering self-love can be long, winding, and demanding. Across the rough waters of this journey lies a life waiting for you that is full of joy, love, and happiness. And, because you never get all your work done in this lifetime, things can only get better as you practice staying with yourself time and time again.

12

YOU CAN FIND TRUE LOVE AT LONG LAST!

"In true love, you attain freedom.
When you love, you bring freedom to the person you love.
If the opposite is true, it is not true love.
You must love in such a way that the person you love feels free,
not only on the outside but also inside."

— Thich Nhat Hanh,
True Love: A Practice for Awakening the Heart

WHAT IS IT WE'RE SEEKING WHEN WE WANT TO FIND TRUE LOVE?

You may answer that you want companionship, kindness, respect, fun, a sense of humor, touch, affection, attraction, sexual chemistry, intelligence, wit, play, warmth, hugs, connection, familiarity, shared routines, comfort, and more. All of this is good. It is exactly what we all deserve.

Consider this idea. *Often when we seek love, we want to feel free.* Free from what? Free from fear, loneliness, disconnection, sadness, frustration, anger, anxiety, control by others, boredom, discomfort, and more. We desperately want liberation from our struggle with feeling unworthy, unloved, and alone. Whether in a romantic relationship or not, the feelings of heartbreak, loss, and isolation are painful and feel too great to bear at times. We want freedom from those feelings when they arise, because it sometimes feels like we cannot survive if the pain continues.

From where does true freedom arise? Does it come from relying on others for our sense of worthiness and love? Are we free when we can control our external conditions completely? Some would assert that their rights and freedoms are violated when they are asked to participate in actions that benefit the entire community. "Don't tread on me." Yet, if our sense of freedom depends on others' actions, can you consider it to be true freedom?

Loving yourself and finding inner grounding and peace is the path to true freedom and liberation. The truth is that the circumstances around us are always coming and going. Things are arising, abiding, and passing away. We will feel sadness and loss, happiness and gain. When we can rediscover and cultivate our own ability to love ourselves, to stay with ourselves again and again, we will find true freedom from constant struggle.

Again, I will never tell you that this is an easy path. When you reach one level of understanding self-love and freedom, you will find that there will still be more times of discomfort, struggle, and breakthroughs to deeper understanding and joy. Things will continue to get better and better when you commit to staying with yourself and returning to yourself and your love.

THE STEPS TO FINDING TRUE LOVE

After relating to you my story of love, loss, and redemption, I shared with you the steps you can take to remember who you are and to learn how to stay with yourself. The first essential step is to slow down. In Chapter 4, we looked at how hard we find it to slow down in our overcrowded and overwhelming daily lives. Slowing your life down will require you to make some decisions about what is most important to you. You learned about the limbic system and the higher functioning prefrontal cortex and how you can move into a *top-down* manner of living. You can slow down your mind and thinking to observe your feelings and thoughts to develop metacognition. You can then cultivate the ability to pause, reflect, and respond skillfully to yourself and others. Cultivating metacognition is a necessary step to rediscovering your love for yourself.

In Chapter 5, we explored the necessity of taking care of your physical body. A first priority must be attending to your gut health. Taking care of your gut health will automatically start to decrease the danger signals of inflammation to your brain. Restoring and maintaining your gut/ brain axis will give you greater access to the mental clarity and energy needed to make good choices for yourself. When the body and mind are inflamed and out of balance, it is much more challenging, perhaps impossible, to do the hard work of reconnecting with your deep love for yourself. We reviewed some first necessary steps to heal your gut. Consider consulting with a functional medicine practitioner to have an additional evaluation, with stool and nutrient testing to optimize your health.

In Chapter 6, we considered the many ways that we run away from ourselves. We looked at how you may be abandoning yourself in the emotional, physical, financial, organizational, spiritual, and relational aspects of your life. Recognizing how you may be chronically leaving yourself and your needs is necessary to learning how to stay with yourself and your feelings. Write out a list of how you are treating yourself in these areas of life. Be honest with yourself. Facing our discomfort with how we are living is essential to rediscovering how to love yourself.

In Chapter 7, we examined in considerable depth how to stay with ourselves. We learned that you must be willing to endure pain and take responsibility for caring for your feelings. It may take a great deal of time and experience before you are ready to do this. However, when you continually relinquish responsibility for your feelings, you will continue to struggle in frequent and familiar cycles of distress and dissatisfaction. Become aware of the false beliefs that have developed to help you avoid discomfort and defend yourself against feelings of pain and anguish. Increasing awareness and understanding will provide you with the opportunity for internal dialogue concerning the self-abandoning behaviors that you have identified. Pause to reflect when you feel pain and discomfort. Ask yourself, *What is the most loving action that I can take for myself in this moment?* When you have developed the ability to slow down, you will be better able to act lovingly toward yourself, to stay with yourself.

In Chapter 8, we discussed the importance of defining boundaries to protect and stay with yourself. You learned how to define your personal boundaries by tuning in to how you feel in different situations when asked or forced to do something. Begin to practice bravery by clearly stating your boundaries and needs to others. When you are ready with your clear self-love and well-defined boundaries, you can start to explore what you require and need in a romantic relationship. When firmly grounded in your self-love, you can be much clearer about what you want and need and can share your love with another freely and joyfully.

In Chapter 9, we delved into dating as a practice in self-love, courage, wisdom, and kindness. There are many ways to practice moving out of your comfort zone to discover endless opportunities to grow and expand, and dating is one great way to practice. Start from a place of inspiration about who you are. After you rediscover your own love and joy, you can share that beauty with others. Inspire yourself with the love stories of others. Do not start dating until you feel consistently happy and loving with yourself. Then shine your light brightly! If you are pursuing online dating, create a profile reflecting who you are, what you value, and what you want. When you choose to meet someone, use the framework of The Anatomy of Trust (BRAVING) taught by Brené Brown. Keeping your boundaries and developing trust will allow you to build great relationships. Dare greatly and date greatly!

Finally, in Chapter 10, I reminded you that you must always be the first one in line to receive your love. We can rediscover self-love and then lose it again when we are feeling pressured, whether in a new or an ongoing relationship. How do we maintain our self-care and love? We make great friends with and make room for our self-care practices. We maintain the connection with our friends and family. We cultivate an ongoing connection to nature and the outdoors. We move through life mindfully and joyfully, developing a regular meditation practice. These routines reinforce and strengthen your ability to stay with yourself always.

MY DEEPEST WISH FOR YOU

You have the freedom to choose the life you want. Have the first moment of awareness that you do have the power to make different choices for yourself, as frightening and threatening as making these choices may seem at first. Step by step, you will begin to see and believe what is possible. You will become the author of the life you want to live. You deserve to feel good and to be free. These were my concluding thoughts to my readers in *Physician, Care for Thyself.* I smile as I note that my intention for you and everyone else has not changed since writing this first book.

There are many shared themes between that book and this one. As I travel further and further along the path to remembering who I am, I uncover more insight into how I had unwittingly blocked myself from my own love and freedom. I know how difficult it can be to struggle with yourself. For this reason, I am committed to sharing all that I have learned along the way. My deepest wish for you is to find true love and self-awareness.

You must love yourself in such a way that you feel free! This is your birthright. You were born and created to live joyfully and to love deeply. Stay with yourself. Abandon self-abandonment! When you embrace yourself with your love, the world will open in ways that you could never have imagined, in every new moment. You will experience love, joy, and beauty beyond measure. Ready? Let's go!

ACKNOWLEDGMENTS

Ever on the edge of discovery is where I always want to be! Writing this second book was a direct follow-up to writing my first, *Physician, Care for Thyself*. I have been in this goopy place of self-examination for most of my adult life. Who am I? Why am I the way that I am? Will I ever love myself just as I am? How do I get there from here? I wrote this second book in service to myself, and others like myself, who have forgotten who they are. Under all the layers of hurt, habits, and conditioning, we are all luminous beings of love and joy. I am grateful for the opportunity and privilege to write this book.

To my dear parents, Wendy and Bill Wei – you have been with me through all of it, supporting and loving me through every choice and decision I have made. Mom, you are one of the strongest and kindest people I know. Thank you for all that you have taught me, and for providing for me with the deepest love that you know.

To Ben and David, my Dearest Ones – I am content to know that you are happy and are living lives full of wonder and discovery. Thank you for all that you are and are ever becoming. You are my true loves, ever and always.

To the Author Incubator Team:

Special thanks to Dr. Angela Lauria, CEO and Founder of The Author Incubator, for believing in me and my message. Two years ago, if told that I would be the author of two books, I would never have believed such a story. Only through the devoted work and dedication of Angela Lauria are my books possible today. To my Developmental and Managing Editor, Erika Parsons – thank you for your support, wisdom, and encouragement. You are one of the many sister-warriors that I have been so fortunate to meet on this amazing journey! Many more thanks to everyone behind the scenes at TAI, who make all this possible for so many.

ABOUT THE AUTHOR

Dr. Jessica Wei is a board-certified Ob-Gyn who had the great privilege and honor to take care of thousands of women for seventeen years, during their pregnancies and during every phase of life from ages ten to ninety-five. Her conventional medical training began at the University of Virginia School of Medicine, after completing her undergraduate and graduate studies. She then completed her residency in Obstetrics and Gynecology with the University of Connecticut School of Medicine. She practiced very successfully as an Ob-Gyn in private practice in Connecticut.

Over the years, as she listened carefully to thousands of women's stories of their lives and their bodies, she began to realize the many limitations of a conventional medical practice. She often felt that she did not have the proper tools to help women discover their true health and sense of well-being. And as she devoted her life to helping other women, she began to lose her health and vitality, and almost let her own life completely slip away.

In search of better questions and keys to healing, she completed her fellowship in Integrative Medicine with the Arizona Center for Integrative Medicine, and her certification in Functional Medicine with the Institute for Functional Medicine. After she left her conventional medical practice in 2016, she took the leap and established her functional medicine practice. In 2019, she wrote *Physician, Care for Thyself* as a guide to help others navigate their journey from burnout to happiness. She now works as a telehealth functional medicine doctor.

She lives in West Hartford, Connecticut, with her two fabulous teenaged sons. She loves walking barefoot outside, immersing herself in nature, and finding freedom in each present moment. As she follows her bliss more deeply, she knows that more beauty, joy, and love will continue to manifest.

ABOUT DIFFERENCE PRESS

Difference Press is the exclusive publishing arm of The Author Incubator, an educational company for entrepreneurs – including life coaches, healers, consultants, and community leaders – looking for a comprehensive solution to get their books written, published, and promoted. Its founder, Dr. Angela Lauria, has been bringing to life the literary ventures of hundreds of authors-in-transformation since 1994.

A boutique-style self-publishing service for clients of The Author Incubator, Difference Press boasts a fair and easy-to-understand profit structure, low-priced author copies, and author-friendly contract terms. Most importantly, all of our #incubatedauthors maintain ownership of their copyright at all times.

Let's Start a Movement with Your Message

In a market where hundreds of thousands of books are published every year and are never heard from again, The Author Incubator is different. Not only do all Difference Press books reach Amazon bestseller status, but all of our authors are actively changing lives and making a difference.

Since launching in 2013, we've served over 500 authors who came to us with an idea for a book and were able to write it and get it self-published in less than 6 months. In addition, more than 100 of those books were picked up by traditional publishers and are now available in bookstores. We do this by selecting the highest quality and highest potential applicants for our future programs.

Our program doesn't only teach you how to write a book – our team of coaches, developmental editors, copy editors, art directors, and marketing experts incubate you from having a book idea to being a published, bestselling author, ensuring that the book you create can actually make a difference in the world. Then we give you the training you need to use your book to make the difference in the world, or to create a business out of serving your readers.

Are You Ready to Make a Difference?

You've seen other people make a difference with a book. Now it's your turn. If you are ready to stop watching and start taking massive action, go to http://theauthorincubator.com/apply/.

"Yes, I'm ready!"

OTHER BOOKS BY DIFFERENCE
PRESS

Start a Profitable Business in 90 Days or Less: The Straightforward Business Planning Guide by Dr. Vanity C. Barr-Little
The Secret Art of Non-Toxic Relationships: Journaling Your Way to a Drama-Less Existence by Ana-Maria Figueredo
Break Free from Heart Attack Fear: The Survivor's Guide to Embrace Your Truth, Regain Confidence & Restore Control by Lisa Steele George
Divorce Like a Boss: The Ultimate Tactical Guide to End a Toxic Marriage and Fulfill Your Purpose by Jadinah N. S. Gustave, Esquire
Aligned: The Essential Guide to Feel God's Love and Trust the Answers Within by Pamela Herzer, M.A.
If It's Not One Thing, It's My Mother!: The Journey to Discover and Heal Your Relationship with Your Narcissistic Mother by Vikki Hibberd
Pay Yourself First: The Ultimate Guide to Saving for Life Events by Lynette Hurd
The Depressed Mom's Guide to Freedom: Creating Happiness in Motherhood by Susan Jungermann

Heal from Your Narcissist Ex: The Ultimate Guide to Finding Safety and Sanity by Heather J. Kent

The End of Imposter Syndrome: Face Your Fears and Become a Successful Coach by Carine Kindinger

The Shatterproof Leader: 7 Keys to Lead with Love (and Love It Too) by Patti Rose

Living Life in the Middle: The Caregiver's Guide to Healing, Hope, and Harmony through Multigenerational Living by Patricia Sheveland

Soul Proprietor: The Entrepreneurial Approach to an Unconventional Life by Robin Theiss

A Healer's Journey: The Guide to a Life without Physician Burnout by Subhashie Wijemanne, MD

THANK YOU

Thank you so much for reading *You Can Find True Love: The Essential Guide to Meeting the Love of Your Life*. My deepest wish for you is to connect again with your true love for yourself. As Oscar Wilde once said, "To love oneself is the beginning of a lifelong romance."

I would love to know more about your journey, your dreams, and your thoughts about finding true love. Please keep in touch! You can contact me anytime at www.jessicaweimd.com.

Let's find your true love: the one who wants to laugh and play, and be truly free and happy!

Made in the USA
Middletown, DE
22 April 2021